Managing
Congregations
in a
Virtual Age

Managing Congregations in a
VIRTUAL AGE

JOHN W. WIMBERLY JR.

FORTRESS PRESS
MINNEAPOLIS

MANAGING CONGREGATIONS IN A VIRTUAL AGE

Scripture quotations are from the New Revised Standard Version Bible © 1989 Division of Christian Education of the National Council of the Churches of Christ in the United States of America. Used by permission.

Cover Image: ID 1664900240 © metamorworks | iStock
Cover Design: Marti Naughton

Print ISBN: 978-1-5064-7263-8
Ebook ISBN: 978-1-5064-7264-5

Contents

Preface

I decided to write this book as I saw my consulting clients struggling with and, in most cases, overcoming many of the challenges of virtual management during the pandemic of 2020. The challenge that received the most attention in my congregation-oriented research sources (blogs, religious publications, and online articles) was moving from on-site to online worship, either streamed live or recorded. As a pastor of forty years, however, I realized that the worship transition would be relatively easy compared to the issues related to virtually managing staff and volunteers. Why? Because managing staff and volunteers is always the most difficult thing in ministry. Sadly, it receives little attention, which probably explains why congregations often suffer from less than stellar management.

Since I am not currently a pastor, I decided to use two primary resources of information for this book. I read a lot of literature from the business world on virtual management. Most large businesses have an international dimension today, and I knew there would be a lot of research going back over a decade. I was not disappointed. Google "manage virtually," and you can have some fun and be informed by what appears. For the most part, I focused on research from major business schools.

However, I found many informative articles in newspapers and online magazines.

After I had a good grasp of the issues related to virtual management as understood in the business community, I interviewed congregationally based clergy and staff, two denominational bishops, a few judicatory staff, several chief executive officers of nonprofits, and several international businesspeople. They provided a wealth of information, giving me specific examples of what they were doing, what worked, and what did not. I am extremely grateful to them. I list them below.

I would also like to acknowledge the insights of my colleagues at Congregational Consulting (https://www .congregationalconsulting.org/). Our monthly discussions are an inspiration and fed many of my conclusions in this book. A special thank you to Dan Hotchkiss, who urged me to make sure I did not confine my research to those who manage but included the perspective of those managed. The latter played a crucial role in my recommendations on management.

I am blessed with one of the finest editors in the United States. Beth Gaede has been an invaluable source of help. She sees things I do not, asks questions I do not, and makes suggestions about issues to probe deeply. For this book, she has been particularly insightful, since she does the bulk of her work at home. When I said things that did not match her experiences, I had to defend my position! Having to defend a position before it ends up in a book is always a good thing. Beth was and is a godsend to me and all her authors. I am also grateful for the work of Scribe Inc., who did the final copyediting and formatting. They improved the final product in many ways.

I thank all the congregations I have served as both a pastor and a consultant. I hope I have helped them somewhat. For sure, they have taught me much about ministry.

Finally, I thank my incredibly supportive wife, Phyllis. I do not know how many times I said, "I'm almost done," and she replied, "Not to worry."

To my readers, please know the deep respect I hold for you as congregational leaders. Your work is so crucial to healing our polarized society and serving as a font of grace-filled love for your members and communities. Thank you.

Ellen Agler, executive director, Temple Sinai, Washington, DC

Leigh Bond, senior pastor, Beargrass Disciples of Christ Church, Louisville, Kentucky

Jerry Cannon, senior pastor, C. N. Jenkins Memorial Presbyterian Church, Charlotte, North Carolina

Hal Chorpenning, pastor, Plymouth Congregational UCC Church, Fort Collins, Colorado

Laura Cunningham, senior pastor, Western Presbyterian Church, Washington, DC

Mindy Douglas, senior pastor, First Presbyterian Church, Durham, North Carolina

Edward Harding, senior pastor, Prince George's Community Church, Prince George's County, Maryland

Peter James, senior pastor, Vienna Presbyterian Church, Vienna, Virginia

Shannon Kershner, senior pastor, Fourth Presbyterian Church, Chicago, Illinois

Boo McCready, director of Children's Spiritual Life, Church of the Atonement, Overland Park, Kansas

Arlene Nehring, senior pastor, Eden United Church of Christ, Hayward, California

Karen Oliveto, bishop of the Mountain Sky Conference of the United Methodist Church, Denver, Colorado

Rabbi Jonathan Roos, senior rabbi, Temple Sinai,
    Washington, DC
Craig Satterlee, bishop of the North/West Lower Michigan
    Synod of the Evangelical Lutheran Church in America,
    Lansing, Michigan
Scott Schenkelberg, chief executive officer, Miriam's Kitchen
    for the Homeless, Washington, DC
Zac Sturm, senior pastor, Church of the Atonement,
    Overland Park, Kansas
David Taylor, international businessperson, Arlington,
    Virginia
Beth Taylor, international businessperson, Arlington,
    Virginia
Kris Thompson, chief executive officer, Calvary Women's
    Services, Washington, DC
Cynthia Vermillion-Foster, director of member services,
    Unity Worldwide Ministries, Lee's Summit, Missouri

Introduction

In addition to the deaths, illnesses, job loss, and other tragic realities caused by the arrival of COVID-19 in early 2020, the global workplace was transformed. From Cape Town to Caracas, Singapore to San Francisco, many workers unexpectedly and suddenly needed to work from home. Instead of commuting from their homes to work, people began commuting from their kitchens to office spaces they had carved out of a spare bedroom, their family room, or a corner of the dining room table. Instead of enjoying the camaraderie of physical interaction with coworkers, they learned to nurture those relationships virtually. Instead of gathering in a conference room to plan, they signed in for a videoconference call.

Of course, for decades, a growing number of people had been working from home by choice. Working remotely has many advantages, ranging from not needing to purchase clothes for work, to increased lifestyle flexibility, and to not having to fend off road-raging commuters. Nonetheless, with the emergence of the pandemic, people were forced to work from home. Many for-profit, nonprofits, and religious congregations were not prepared for the sudden transition from on-site work to their entire staff working remotely. Likewise, many workers were not prepared.

In parts of the business community, employees had been working virtually for many years, so although the sudden and large-scale move to at-home work caused by COVID-19 was unexpected, it was not an unfamiliar experience for some businesses and their employees. For example, stockbrokers have long made trades from homes located far from New York City, people employed by call centers have solved customers' problems from their homes, and sales representatives have operated virtually without visiting the home office.

For faith communities, however, the move to working from home, virtual meetings, and streaming worship services has been much more of an upheaval. Yes, for many years, most pastors and many other staff members have worked from home part of the week. To get away from distractions when I was serving congregations, I always went home to write sermons. Other church leaders have used their homes as quiet spaces for meditation, prayer, and study. Staff working in tech-savvy congregations have been able to access their church-based files (usually located on a server or in the cloud), prepare shared documents such as worship bulletins, monitor financial data, update websites, send out e-blasts, and do other tasks that had previously required being in a central office. However, prior to the COVID-19 crisis, few of us had ever been required to remain in our homes and still engage in and manage an active ministry—everything from worship to pastoral care.

Various aspects of the move to work from home have been difficult. For example, while buildings have been emptied for the most part during the pandemic, they still need to be maintained. Figuring out, from home, what tasks employees and contractors need to take care of has been a challenge. The inability of pastors to visit members in hospitals, nursing homes, and retirement facilities has been frustrating and guilt producing, to say the least. Not having live interaction with a congregation while preaching is a major change. Talk show hosts, comedians, and others who regularly performed to live audiences are talking about how difficult this transition has been.

Fortunately, to help with the challenges of working from home, various forms of technology and productivity tools have made it easier. These resources are not new, however. Many of them have been widely used in the business community for at least a decade. But because they have been underutilized in congregational settings, few congregations or their staff members were prepared to work and carry out ministry exclusively from home, as was required during the pandemic. This book is not about using technology to cope with a pandemic or other disaster, however. Yes, the pandemic alerted me to the need for this book. But my goal is to lay out principles and practices regarding virtual management that will serve congregations well into the future, even as technology and circumstances change.

In this book, we will discuss the pros and cons of work off-site. More specifically, we will focus on how a congregation's governing board and head of staff can manage staff working from home or another remote location, such as a coffee shop, library, community center, and so forth. Fundamental questions need to be explored and answered by staff team leaders, congregational governing bodies, and members.

+ How does one know that a staff person is working?
+ How does one maintain a sense of "team," give appropriate direction to team members, and get needed feedback from them?
+ How will congregants connect with staff members who are not working at the church or synagogue? (It is one thing to drop by the church in search of a staff person. It is a totally different thing to drop by their house!)

- What policies might be needed about the type of work that can be done remotely versus work that needs to be done at the office?
- What support—for example, laptops, printers, high-speed internet connections, and other tools—should a congregation provide for staff members' home offices?
- What changes in office design and use are needed to protect those working in and entering them from future virus outbreaks?

As I address these questions, I will rely not only on research but on interviews I have conducted with senior pastors and rabbis as well as church staff members and congregants.

Changes in Today's Workplace

Fortunately, congregations do not have to invent the work-from-home wheel. The business world can teach us a great deal. Increasingly over the past twenty years, many in the business world have understood and harnessed the power of virtual work. A friend of mine who works for a telecom giant has been working virtually with her team of software developers for fifteen years. While she lives in Washington, DC, everyone else on the team lives in various cities in India. She says she is as personally close to her current teammates as any with whom she has ever been involved. As important, her team is as productive as any she has experienced. Working from home and managing people remotely are not the norms in the business community. However, neither are they unusual. This book will draw heavily on the business community's experience with remote work. Increasing numbers of people working somewhere other than the office is only one aspect of a workplace that has seen multiple changes in the twenty-first century.

Working remotely has allowed people in the United States to move from high-density metropolitan areas to less populated parts of the country. While physically located in a nonurban area, workers from home are closely connected to their home offices, which are typically located in the cities from which they moved. As long as an area has dependable high-speed internet, people can work from their homes most of the time. The *Wall Street Journal* reports, "Among freelancers, nearly four-fifths choose to do so partly because it allows them to work from a location of their choosing, according to a survey by the freelance marketplace Upwork Inc. The survey also found that if freelancing keeps increasing in popularity, people are more likely to move out of urban job centers to places that cater to their lifestyles."[1]

In addition to allowing many people to live where they want, rather than where they must due to work, today's workplace has a number of other fascinating characteristics:

+ Today's workplace is far more diverse. Women, people of color, individuals with disabilities, LGBTQ folks, people within a wide range of ages, and people falling into other demographic characteristics increasingly lead workplaces that previously were led overwhelmingly by white males.

+ Today's workplaces, including some congregations, are empowered by technology. Everything from email to text messaging to videoconferencing to WhatsApp to Twitter dominates the way we communicate within organizations. Servers that can be accessed from anywhere—Dropbox, OneDrive, and other forms of cloud storage—allow workers to quickly share material with their colleagues.

- Dress codes have disappeared in many workplaces. At first, businesses allowed "casual Fridays." Today's workers can go casual pretty much whenever they want.
- Today, employees are often organized in teams. This has increased productivity and placed the focus more on team than individual performance.
- For most of history, there was no way to challenge sexual harassment in the workplace. Today, most organizations have sexual harassment/misconduct policies. Implementing and enforcing them, however, is still a project in process.
- Implicitly, if not explicitly, most workplaces have an eye on global trends. From organizations around the world, we learn what works and does not work.
- The "contract" between workers and employers that kept workers tied to one employer has weakened considerably. Daniel Bortz says, "Today, workers change jobs on average every 4.2 years, according to a recent report (9/2018) on employee tenure from the Bureau of Labor Statistics."[2] These numbers vary a bit by generation. Younger workers today are likely to change jobs many times in their lifetimes, while older workers stay put for longer periods.
- Benefit packages in the workplace have changed, which explains, in part, why younger generations change jobs more often than older folks. While many employers today offer health care options, as of 2018, only 17 percent of private employers offered defined benefit pension plans.[3] In the past, defined benefit pensions and health packages kept many employees tied to their employer. Today, with the widespread use of portable 401(k)-type plans, employees have less to lose by moving to another job. Their retirement savings travel with them.

+ The skill sets needed in the workplace are also changing. According to a Pew Social Trends study, "Employment in jobs requiring average or above-average levels of social skills, such as interpersonal, communications or management skills, increased 83% from 1980 to 2015. Meanwhile, employment in jobs requiring higher levels of analytical skills, such as critical thinking and computer use, increased 77%."[4]

+ Today's employees want to grow vocationally. Employers offering continuing education / skill development are more likely to attract and retain the best employees.

As this list of changes in the workplace reveals, the move toward working from home is part of a rapidly changing work environment for employers and employees alike. These changes have implications for congregations. Congregations that understand shifts in work practices and develop strategies around these challenges will appeal to the "cream of the crop" workers. Congregations managing their staff teams as though it is 1980 will struggle to attract the best.

Overview

In this book, I will lay out the opportunities and challenges of congregational staff increasing the amount of time they work from home. I draw on formal interviews I conducted with clergy serving pastoral-, program-, and larger-size congregations. When asked, "What are your key management approaches?" all of them described very similar core management principles. They also talked about common challenges and opportunities managing and leading their staff teams as they moved to a virtual team reality.

I have not spent a lot of time differentiating the challenges of managing a small pastoral-style congregation from those of a program- or larger-size congregation. While management challenges and opportunities grow in complexity as the size of staff increases, I think core management principles are fundamentally the same at every size. Henry Mintzberg, a recognized giant in the field of management research, has helped me and millions of others understand this reality. The congregation I managed for thirty years grew from a very small pastoral size to program size, from a $100,000 to $900,000 budget. At the time and in retrospect, I didn't and don't think the management opportunities or challenges changed as the church grew, although certain core management principles were more important than others at different times in the growth of the congregation.

I am not saying that books on the challenges of leading and managing different-sized congregations are not valuable. They are. How we apply core management principles should change depending on a congregation's size. On the topic of virtual management in congregations, though, the challenges and opportunities seem to remain very similar regardless of size. As one pastor said to me, "Technology is the great equalizer of congregations. We all use the same tools." Most literature on virtual management in the business community describes similar challenges and opportunities for huge-, medium-, and small-size corporations. Churches of different sizes will also have experiences with virtual management that are similar to one another.

In chapters 1 and 2, we will discuss the basic principles of excellent management. Understanding the fundamentals of management, in general, is required to have any chance of doing an excellent job of managing virtually. We will discuss what we can learn from research in the nonprofit and business communities regarding the principles and practice of management. We will also hear from a number of clergy who are experienced managers and leaders of their congregations.

In chapter 3, we will look at how the principles and practices of management per se can be adapted to principles and practices for virtual management. Relying on the vast literature written about virtual management, this chapter will lay out what have come to be accepted best practices of virtual management, and we will examine the strengths and weaknesses of various approaches being used in the nonprofit, religious, and business communities to manage virtual employees. We will explore what works in the business community that might not work in a congregation and vice versa. Finally, we will discuss the best practices for managing congregation staff in particular, including the increasing number of part-time staffers in congregations who are replacing full-time workers. With a good grasp of basic management practices, we will examine the unique opportunities virtual management has for managing (1) full-time staff who want to work away from the church offices and (2) part-time staff who spend little time in the building.

In chapter 4, we will move deeper into the challenges and opportunities of working from home and managing virtually. We will discuss common concerns that I hear raised when the subject of working at home is discussed: How do we know our staff are working? Is it healthy for employees to merge home and workspaces? How can ministry performance be measured, given the ambiguity of outcomes such as spiritual growth or inspiring worship? How do we create a sense of being a team and accomplishing shared performance goals when people are rarely together in the church building? As we move to working from home, are we leaving behind the employees who are not tech savvy and do not want to become tech savvy or who have no desire to work from home?

In chapter 5, we consider the implications of what I predict will be an ongoing hybrid model of work (combining some home and some office work). What tools are needed to work at home and manage virtually, including a number of technical issues? For example, should the congregation provide employees with the required hardware and software to work at home (e.g., laptops, printers, software)? What will be the cost of setting up a server or a cloud account that will store shared files as well as serve as the home base for a virtual network? What kind of 24/7 tech support will be necessary for people working at home? The pandemic made everyone aware that most workplaces are not healthy when it comes to the control of viruses, for example. What will healthy workplaces look like in the future?

We will work through questions commonly asked by congregational leadership and members as they consider a hybrid approach to staff work and management. In my experience, congregations tend to have members who fall into two groups: (1) those who intuitively trust that their staff members are diligent, hard workers and (2) those who are less trusting and wonder whether staff are doing everything required of them or stretching themselves to work beyond what is required. Increasing staff members' work away from the church offices may fuel the concerns of group 2. This chapter will discuss how to ensure that those who are less trusting don't derail the transition of staff to do more work from home. How does a congregation make a transparent switch from expecting staff to be in the church office from nine to four o'clock to designating staff office hours but otherwise allowing them to work wherever they please? Without an orderly, transparent shift, the less-trusting members will be more concerned about whether their staff is working hard enough and is accessible, whether working on-site or at home.

I stated earlier that most congregations are not very familiar with staff working from home and managing staff virtually.

That being said, many congregations did it with great skill as the time of quarantine descended on the United States during the COVID-19 pandemic. Staff teams that were used to thrashing things out in face-to-face staff meetings were able to meet virtually to assemble and produce online-streaming worship services in, literally, a matter of weeks. In many congregations, they had no experience with streaming worship or YouTube channels. However, working from home, managing tasks and people from home, staff members got their congregation's worship online with startling speed. So we can do it! Hopefully, this book will enable congregations to achieve even higher levels of performance as they implement a hybrid model of work and develop best practices for managing and nurturing workers in the office and those working at home.

1

Managing People

Increasingly, seminaries offer a class devoted to leadership, a well-researched and much-written-about topic. They should. Clergy are leaders in their congregations, larger faith communities, and hopefully, local communities. But how many seminaries have classes on management? If they do have such a class, how many students choose it as an elective? As surely as clergy serving a congregation must be leaders, they also need to be managers.

Some people are born managers, and that God-given talent may be enough for many situations. But even natural managers are wise to read and think about best practices for managers. For those who are not natural managers, the lack of management knowledge and skill will derail a career and the life of a congregation—every time.

While thousands of great books have been written on leadership, and many clergy avidly devour them, precious few helpful books on management are available. The best, in my opinion, is the short book *Managing* by Canadian management expert and professor Henry Mintzberg. Given that it was written in 2009, the book's only shortfall is understandable: it has too little information about the way technology has affected the task of management. We will attempt to fill that hole in this book.

The difference between leadership and management is relatively straightforward. Leaders lay out visionary direction for a congregation, while managers do the nitty-gritty work of getting a congregation from point A to point B to realize the vision. The thoughts of leaders sometimes seem to drop out of the heavens; the thoughts of managers rise out of the realities of the congregation's daily life. For example, Martin Luther King Jr. cast the vision. Fred Shuttlesworth, Diane Nash, and others organized a movement.

Some larger congregations have the financial wherewithal to hire a business manager, and very large congregations often have a designated "executive pastor" who frees other pastors on the staff from many administrative duties. Even in these congregations, though, lead or senior clergy must manage the overall program of the congregation as well as a core staff team and a core group of lay leaders. There is no escaping the task. The management principles in this chapter will help clergy and lay leaders alike, regardless of their position on a church staff or the size of their congregation. Whether one is a pastor managing a small staff in a pastoral-size congregation, a layperson managing a team of volunteers, or a senior pastor with five staff reports, the techniques needed to be an effective manager are remarkably similar.

A major premise of this book is that management is management—whether the manager is working with a staff on-site, remotely by phone or written direction, or virtually with the help of video technology, smartphones, and email. Each of these management scenarios has its own peculiarities, but they all rely on the same basic principles. Chapters 1 and 2 focus on management per se before we move to virtual management in chapter 3.

The Tyranny of Monday Morning

I like to talk with congregational lay leaders and clergy about the "tyranny of Monday morning." As clergy, we experience a spiritual and emotional "high" as we lead Sunday worship, coming close to our God and congregants in a powerful, mystical way. I have led lots of groups, retreats, and community meetings but have never experienced anything comparable to the power of worshiping God. Sunday afternoon we bask in the glow of the Sunday-morning experience. Even when my favorite sports teams lose on Sunday, the defeat does not bring me all the way down. But then comes Monday morning! On Sunday, we lead beautiful worship services that lift us toward the heavens. On Monday morning, we descend from the mountaintop to plow the fields in the valleys where ministry happens.

During my years as a pastor, I liked to get into the office around seven o'clock in the morning, before my secretary, janitor, or anyone else arrived. In the silence of my office, I could go over the attendance sheets from the pew pads, looking for the names and contact information of Sunday's visitors. I could look at my schedule for the week ahead. I could pull up the lectionary and read the Scripture passages for next Sunday's sermon.

Less than twenty-four hours from Sunday's worship, I moved from the sublime to the mundane matters that make or break a ministry, matters requiring management skills. Managing the life of the congregation seized control of my agenda and life. *The toilet that leaked in the men's bathroom has to be fixed, I thought, and do not forget to remind the janitor that members are complaining on Sundays about insufficient toilet paper in the bathrooms. The bulletin for next week must be created. A staff meeting needs to be led. The budget has to be reviewed. The associate pastor needs a new printer (Why did he tell me instead of ordering it himself?). Plans*

need to be made to cover for the secretary's upcoming vacation. The
Monday-morning list went on and on and on.

Laura A. Hill, professor at the Harvard Business School,
has studied first-time managers. More than a few of them said
something like this: "I thought I would be gaining control when
I became a manager. Instead, I found that I was being controlled
by my job!"[1] So it is for clergy. We had a lot of expectations about
what leading faith communities would be like. Few of us, I wager,
envisioned the tyranny of Monday morning.

Our management responsibilities as clergy make it challenging to remain focused on the bigger, macro issues at the heart
of effective leadership—even to manage the implementation of
strategic priorities. As a pastor whose congregation engaged in
three strategic-planning processes over my thirty-year tenure
at Western Presbyterian Church in Washington, DC, I always
felt challenged to retain strategic focus as a leader while making
sure the staff and I tended to all the management tasks. Instead
of building and expanding a house as clergy and lay leaders, too
often, we are putting out fires that threaten the frame of the house.

In my discussions with clergy, I hear the time spent on managing the mundane to be a recurring frustration. We want to lead.
We want to be change agents. But we find ourselves enmeshed
in the everyday details of managing programs, people, buildings,
and finances. The management needs of the congregations we
serve are not going away, however. The only way to improve the
situation is to become better managers.

Busting a Myth about Managers

So what do most of us conjure up when we imagine the master
manager? Before I started studying management, I believed, like
many others, that outstanding managers are cool, calm, collected
individuals who sit in their offices making data-based, strategic

plan–oriented decisions. Managers are in control—of budgets, employees, strategies, and so forth. They create order out of chaos, setting up orderly systems to make sure that chaos never rears its ugly head again in their realm. Or so I thought.

Mintzberg, Hill, and other management scholars spend literally entire days following top managers around. What they have found is that these women and men are almost the opposite of the stereotype. When describing the actual, rather than the mythological, daily activity of managers, scholars use terms like *brevity, fragmentation, interruptions, surprises,* and *dashing around all the time.* Sounds like the day of a clergyperson to me!

Understanding that the stereotype of the calm manager is not only misleading but fundamentally wrong is key to becoming an effective manager. It will also reduce our guilt about not having everything under control. Management is not about eliminating chaos but about being in the middle of it *and* helping an organization move toward its goals. Too often we see phone calls, emails, texts, and meetings as pulling us away from work. The effective manager, however, sees them as essential work.

Mintzberg and others have found that given the inevitable chaos in most organizations, the skills needed to be a great manager are more about the mental approach to management than management tricks. Rabbi Ed Friedman talked about the need for clergy to be a nonanxious presence in their congregations.[2] While I have never been convinced there is such a thing as a "nonanxious" human being, clergy certainly can aim to be a low-anxiety presence in their congregations. Lowering the anxiety level in our congregations around management and other issues can have a huge positive influence.

Being nonanxious does not mean being in control, however. It means not being hyperanxious when things are out of control. As described by Friedman and, in different terminology, by Mintzberg, non- or less-anxious managers will not overreact to surprises, miscalculations, or disorder by becoming hyperanxious or unnerved. Instead, managers who have their anxiety levels under control will be able to think clearly and problem solve.

I have been proud of the US religious community during the COVID-19 pandemic. During the crisis, for perfectly understandable reasons, the anxiety of the American populace went through the ceiling. From what I saw, the response of the religious community was not overly anxious. For example, when it immediately became clear that in-person worship was not possible, congregations managed the movement to online worship experiences relatively calmly and quickly. Yes, figuring out the technology took a lot of running around, head scratching, and consulting. However, such efforts in a time of chaos were a sign of effective management.

In times of crisis, such as COVID-19, great managers methodically and calmly incorporate as many differing viewpoints as feasible into the decision-making process. Doris Kearns Goodwin's book *Team of Rivals* makes this point about Lincoln. In the midst of the most chaotic upheaval in the nation's history, Lincoln calmly (at least outwardly) sought out as many voices, friendly and opposed, as possible before making decisions. His calm pursuit of the best approach was key to managing and leading what many considered an unmanageable nation.

Amid the chaos of COVID-19, economic collapse, and massive protests of racial injustice, congregations have provided a calm, stable, often virtual space for their members and others. They did so even as they reconfigured and managed their organizational lives. Talking with congregational leaders, I have sensed that part of their success is the result of a new openness to try strategies that they might not have embraced in other times.

One thing we can learn from congregations' responses to the pandemic is that great managers are not birthed in MBA programs. Management is learned on the job. Yes, a person seeking to manage effectively should read books and articles on the subject by scholars like Friedman, Mintzberg, and Hill. However, ultimately, anything learned in a book must be relearned in the soil of one's ministry. We learn to manage by managing and mismanaging. We do something right and remember it for the next time. We make mistakes and learn from them. The important things we learn probably have more to do with intangibles, such as anxiety and interpersonal interactions, than tangibles, such as spreadsheets and financial reports.

One of the things I had to learn when I first became a solo pastor was that I was totally micromanaging our congregation's wonderful janitor, Gaston Paige. My anxiety level was high as we started a major feeding program for the homeless, inviting about three hundred people into the church each morning for breakfast. I was terrified things would not run well, our members would turn against the program, and we would have to shut the program down, depriving our guests of a healthy meal and crucial social services. With an overwhelming number of start-up issues to tend to, rather than inviting Gaston more deeply into the decision-making about how to clean the kitchen and large dining area, I started issuing him instructions. Gaston, much smarter than I, did exactly as I instructed instead of following his own instincts and knowledge about how to get the job done. The rooms got cleaned, but the process took far more time than was necessary. I finally realized that Gaston needed to manage the cleaning, and I needed to support him. Once I figured that out, Gaston and I began to build a relationship of trust and friendship that lasted thirty years. To be clear, I kept making suggestions, and Gaston kept rightly rejecting most of them. But over time, I realized he was the expert, not me. Our management relationship became a team dialogue rather than a managerial monologue. The effectiveness of a lower-anxiety approach to cleaning taught me a lesson I applied to other challenges as time went by. I also learned that to

manage was not to be in control. In the chaos of starting a large
feeding program for the homeless, I discovered that the key was
staying focused on the vision (providing a good meal in a safe,
caring space).

Who and What Are We Managing?

Focusing obsessively on problem-solving is a seductive management temptation. However, problems flow from issues in
the system from whence they come. If we do not deal with the
source of the problem—the system—the problem will just keep
coming back. A congregation is a large system with multiple
systems within it. A typical congregation will have subsystems,
such as staff, leaders, participants in programmatic areas (spiritual
growth, mission, worship, and the like), demographic groups
(younger people with families, retired people, youth and children,
and so forth), and perhaps groups of members who form what
amounts to a system around particular theological or political
views. Effective management requires a broad understanding
of the overall system, the subsystems, and how they interact.
Effective managers possess broad knowledge of the complete
system, understanding the way the pieces of a system interact
and impact each other. They are experts at helping the parts of
the system work together to achieve the greater purposes of the
congregation. An effective manager connects the dots within
the system so staff and volunteers understand their work in rela-
tion to the greater purpose.

For example, consider two subsystems that exist in almost
every congregation: maintenance/cleaning and education.
An effective manager understands that without clean, well-
maintained rooms, the morale of the teachers and students will be
undermined, and parents will be unhappy. Therefore, the manager
makes sure the maintenance and cleaning staff listen carefully to

the needs of the teachers and then do the work requested. The effective manager also recognizes that maintenance and cleaning staff are the experts at cleaning and ensures they have the tools and supplies they need.

The manager will be sure to connect the work of both the teachers and the maintenance staff to the larger purpose of the congregation. For many congregations, a primary purpose is to attract families with children. To achieve such a purpose, the classrooms need to be safe and clean. When I have been asked to give congregations advice on how to attract families with children, the first thing I ask is, "Are your classrooms attractive, safe, and clean?" If not, families will go elsewhere. Managers add value when they know and help others know how maintenance and teaching work together to create a congregational system that is appealing to families with children.

One way to frame managers' jobs in a congregation is to think about the many discrete areas where they will need to develop expertise. Management scholars use different names to describe these key areas of managerial expertise, but I will use the following interconnected categories:

+ people
+ information
+ resources
+ workflow
+ performance
+ culture

The rest of this chapter is about the "people" category. As managers, we can keep the financial books in order and hit many performance measures. However, if we do not manage people well, it won't make much difference.

People

Managing people is always the most challenging and rewarding part of being a manager. It's challenging because every person requires a slightly different approach from a manager; it's rewarding because few things are more satisfying than seeing a staff person or volunteer develop and succeed. In this section, we will discuss a few of the many things to consider when managing people. When we get to managing people virtually, we will see how the task increases in difficulty.

Hiring

Leigh Bond, senior pastor of Beargrass Disciples of Christ Church in Louisville, Kentucky, summarized his key management strategy succinctly: "Hire all-stars."[3] Indeed, finding talented, highly motivated, hardworking, creative individuals to work as staff should be a high priority for any congregation. I always warn congregations, "Don't hire someone just to fill a hole, because if you hire the wrong person, the hole will become an abyss!" High-quality staff, obviously, make the management task much easier. The problem is simple: How does one find and recognize them?

My father, a Presbyterian pastor, readily acknowledged that he made several bad hires for the associate pastor position at churches he served. He hired some wonderful individuals to serve as associate pastors but watched in dismay as they turned out to be low performers or bad fits. I used to wonder if they were truly bad hires or poorly managed by him. After talking with numerous people who are more objective about my father than I, I concluded that he was a bad evaluator in the hiring process, although the successful performance of most staff members, including one longtime associate pastor, indicated he had some excellent management skills. Whatever the causes, the mistakes in associate pastor hires hindered the ministry of the congregations he served.

The associate who was a sensational fit loved being an associate pastor, having no desire to be a head of staff, and had an excellent work history as an associate. He loved and was excellent at his areas of work: Christian education and music ministry. He was extroverted, a good team player, and a hard worker but not a workaholic in a system that valued these traits.

Why did my dad miss on two and hit the jackpot on a third? In both cases, I think he undervalued the importance of his congregation's culture and failed to ask enough questions about the person's skills. The "bad" hires were not bad people or even bad associate pastors. They were bad fits. One was flashy in a midwestern culture that valued humility. Another was introverted in a culture that valued extroversion. In addition, my dad and the search committee failed to adequately assess whether the candidates would be productive in their assigned ministry—or at least open to efforts to help them improve. One was new to ministry, so there was no way to find out about his performance in prior congregations, while the other person convinced the search committee that his problems in a previous congregation were its fault, not his. The jackpot associate pastor, Al Fryer, was such a good fit for the congregation's culture and so skilled that the search committee and my dad could not make a mistake!

Yes, "fit" can be difficult to discern. But it's not impossible. For example, your congregation and its staff culture may be one where there is a lot of healthy conflict. Some people do not like even healthy conflict. A conflict-averse person would not be a good fit for a staff that views constructive conflict as productive. Your culture may expect people to speak up if they see something wrong, so the congregation should not hire a person who is reticent to express their views, fearing that they might sound like a complainer. Your culture may value timeliness and punctuality and therefore should avoid hiring a person about whom former employers observe, "You'll get quality work, but you'll have to wait for it."

Of course, critical to a successful hire is not just a culture match but also how well a candidate's skills match the congregation's needs. In the next section of this chapter, we'll discuss expectations. If managers make expectations clear in a job description, it increases the likelihood that a new hire will be a good fit. If a manager is less than crystal clear about what skills and experience are needed to do a particular job, good luck.

Understanding what type of person fits and who does not in a congregation and its staff is a crucial part of the hiring process. A congregation and its staff need to be able to accurately describe their culture and determine what elements of it are essential for a good fit. I find that having the current staff talk about their team culture is an essential prehiring discussion. Indeed, things about the culture that were implicit may become explicit to the staff in such discussions. Exit interviews with departing staff members are also an excellent source of information about a congregational culture.

Many experts also advise that we not focus totally on skills. We need to ask, Are they talented? Dictionary.com describes talent as "a special, natural ability or aptitude" and "a capacity for achievement, success."[4] In other words, a talented person has the ability to take a specific skill set to a higher level. Asking candidates to give specific high points from their careers may help a manager discern if a person can soar above their skill set: "What do you consider your greatest success in ministry?" "When have you exceeded your own expectations of what was possible?" Questions such as these will help you know where candidates set the bar for themselves—high or low. If the example a candidate gives isn't all that "high," one will have gained some important information. Great hires require evaluating, not just accepting, the information we are given by a candidate.

We also need to talk with people beyond the references given to us by candidates. Who supplies a possible future employer with a bad reference? Certainly, the US government doesn't. Because Western Church was located in Washington, DC, the Secret Service or FBI regularly came to me about a church member who was applying for a position. Their last question was always, "Is there anyone else we should talk to about this person?" With that question, they were acknowledging the need to move beyond the references supplied by an applicant to other sources of feedback regarding the person's behavior. An FBI friend told me that this is where they get most of their helpful information.

Another valuable practice for hiring staff came from one of my mentors. When conducting a job search, she recruited church members who had experience in the work area under consideration to help with interviews and the final decision. For example, if the church was looking for an administrative assistant, she found some members who were themselves or who worked closely with administrative assistants. If looking for someone to do communications and marketing, she found members with experience in those areas. These small interviewing teams, made up of people who knew what they were doing, rarely made a bad hire. Actually, a best practice for just about anything in ministry is to find people who know what they are doing!

When hiring, another legitimate consideration is whether the staff team and congregation need to be shaken up a bit. In some businesses, such as technology, staffers who challenge the conventional wisdom of an organization, referred to as "disrupters" in some management literature, are viewed positively. In other organizations, they are viewed negatively. I think Pope Leo X would agree that Martin Luther was most definitely a disrupter, as were Susan B. Anthony and Martin Luther King Jr. Spending time discerning whether a congregation and staff need a disrupter in their midst is worth the effort. Many congregations today can use a staff person who is not afraid of challenging the status quo. Indeed, if I asked my staff team and lay leaders whether they would like a "disrupter" on the staff and they all said "No!" in unison, I would be, almost immediately, tempted to hire one. I would, however, warn the potential new hire what I was asking them to be and do.

It is impossible to overstate the importance of hiring. Laura Cunningham, the senior pastor of Western Church in Washington, DC, says she puts in a lot of time before hiring a person—evaluating the current staff and congregational culture before interviewing candidates, checking references, finding people who are not references who know the candidate and will speak candidly about the person, and making sure the job description has clear expectations. Her emphasis on the hiring process has enabled the congregation to hire several stellar staff members. How much time are you and your congregation devoting to the hiring process?

Expectations about a Job and Performance

Not too long ago, I consulted with an organization's central office staff. As I interviewed each staff person individually, it quickly became clear that staff had very little idea what they were supposed to do individually or how their work fit into the bigger picture. Sure, the communications person knew he was supposed to work on communications, the accountant knew she was supposed to keep the books, and so on. But beyond that, the job expectations were vague. Was his communications department supposed to focus on being cutting-edge, cost-efficient, or conventional? Was the audience for the team's communications within the organization or external? Were communications supposed to be conveyed via the website, e-blasts, hard copies, or all? The lack of clarity regarding job expectations also revealed that individual work was not explicitly linked to the larger stated mission or purpose of the organization.

While students of management universally agree that every employee needs to be explicitly linked to an organization's overall purpose, they increasingly debate the value of managing and working toward tightly defined performance measures that a worker is expected to meet. Some argue that performance measures can limit rather than expand a worker's vision of their job by focusing them totally on microaccomplishments. Yes, managers and those they manage need to start with clear expectations of their specific roles and responsibilities if they are to be successful. But equally important is how a staff person's work relates to the broader mission of the congregation. When the expectations for every job relate to the purpose or mission of a congregation, we prevent areas of ministry from becoming isolating silos in a ministry. We evaluate the success of a congregation based on performance measures for an overall ministry, not silo by silo or individual performance measure by individual performance measure.

I know of a school system where most of the teachers are given high annual performance review ratings. Very few teachers get below-average ratings. And yet many of the students in the school system are doing very poorly on standardized exams. The system is failing even as individual parts of the system are deemed to be successful. If individual performance was evaluated in terms of the overall school system's success, one might see quite different dynamics. Teachers would be incentivized to suggest ways to improve the overall system rather than being content with the quality of their own classes. Managers would be incentivized to listen to teachers, students, and parents so the overall system improved.

A pastor may be given a performance measure to "preach inspiring, motivating sermons." She may succeed spectacularly in achieving the performance measure. But if the performance measure for the congregation is growth in membership and the congregation is declining in membership, what does that tell us? It tells me that inspiring, motivating sermons are not the key to congregational growth in this particular congregation. Obviously, I do not want the pastor to stop preaching great sermons. But if we want to grow the congregation, we need to look elsewhere for strategies. The great sermons may also need to be linked to an additional congregational purpose, such as the spiritual growth of its members.

Performance measures can be misleading when applied narrowly to areas of ministry. It is fairly common to find expectations for a music ministry related to producing beautiful music in worship. As a result, the people producing the music can live in a music silo and not worry about how the rest of the ministry is faring. I observe this in congregation after congregation. Clients regularly say, "We are declining in membership, but we have great music." Apparently, as the RMS *Titanic* sank, the musicians on the ship's deck played beautiful string music. Despite the beautiful music, the ship still sank! If a congregation's goal is to grow its membership, for example, it might consider other strategies to link music to its purpose of growth. One congregation with which I worked recently had a strategy for the congregation's music ministry to produce beautiful music for the community, not just for worship, in hopes that music lovers outside the church might come inside.

When the expectation is that the music ministry will produce inspiring music as part of an overall effort to attract visitors to the church, everything changes. The music ministry now has a stake in engaging people who are not members of the congregation. They can ask, How does music engage first-time visitors to our church? How might our music ministry be active in the community, raising the profile of our congregation? Does our music appeal to the increasingly diverse (racially, generationally, unchurched and otherwise) people who have moved into the surrounding neighborhood? At a minimum, linking music ministry to the overall goals of a congregation to grow will give the musicians a reason to get involved in brainstorming about factors that will contribute to the congregation's growth. The same approach needs to be applied to other traditional programmatic silos in congregations: religious education, youth ministry, and mission. If the purpose of a church is to reach more people with the gospel, we cannot say, "That is someone else's problem. We are doing our job." No, realizing the stated purpose of the congregation is a responsibility for everyone on the staff team, lay leaders, and members.

If every staff person's ultimate goal is the same (the mission/purpose statement of the congregation), a congregation is more likely to make progress toward the goal. If expectations, however, are for each individual staff person to succeed by meeting certain performance measures, regardless of whether the ministry succeeds, the ministry will quickly devolve into silos, some of which are successful, some of which are not. It is a problem that plagues even some of the more successful congregations with which I have consulted.

Aligning staff with the larger goals of a congregation starts before a hiring search begins. The performance expectations of an individual staff person should be linked to the performance expectations of the staff team and congregation as a whole and to strategies for the specific area of ministry. This type of alignment should be addressed explicitly with each candidate for a position as well as during the orientation period for the new employee. Personal performance expectations and their connection to expectations for congregational performance need to be an ongoing topic of conversation between a staff person and supervisor. If not, it is easy for a staff person to become overly focused on individual performance.

When performance measures are explicitly linked to a congregation's purpose statement (the micro linked to the macro), they can be helpful in quantifying what seems unquantifiable. For example, there is an expectation in most congregations that the pastor(s) will preach inspiring sermons, lead informative classes, and manage the affairs of the organization well. But how do we know if our sermons really touched any hearts or changed any behaviors? How do we know if a class had any transformative impact on the participants? How do we know if the time we spend on administration helps the congregation be more effective? Without some performance measurements, we are always left wondering whether we are accomplishing something. As the classic saying goes, "You can't manage what you can't measure."

I am routinely asked, "How can we measure such seemingly imprecise outcomes?" My response: try. As I have seen congregations create performance measures, they have succeeded more times than not. The result is worth the effort.

Some pastors use what amount to focus groups to evaluate sermons. They gather a group of people to get feedback on the quality of their preaching. A performance measure for a religious education class might involve the type of brief survey widely used in higher education to evaluate classes and instructors at the end of a semester. Is a class attracting or losing participants? A performance measure for administration might be linked to staying within the budget or targeted improvements in cleaning and maintenance. Evaluating performance can be done, and using specific measures helps us see whether we are meeting expectations.

The goal of performance measures should be to encourage staffers to take entrepreneurial, innovative approaches to their work that also help realize the congregation's purpose. If, in attempting to reach a performance measure, workers discover a more effective way to achieve the expectation or even discover something that calls into question the expectation itself, supervisors should be open to changing the measure and even the expectation behind the measure. By rewarding creativity and independent thinking, we encourage entrepreneurial approaches to ministry. We are not telling staffers to do their own thing. We are simply asking them to bring their creative ideas and expertise to the staff team for consideration. Miriam's Kitchen for the Homeless in Washington, DC, is a great example of how to do this right.

Respecting the Expertise of Your Workforce

Miriam's Kitchen is a large nonprofit program working to end long-term homelessness in Washington, DC, located at Western Church. From humble beginnings in 1983, it has grown into a widely respected, high-impact program with a budget of over $5 million and a large staff of social workers, advocacy professionals, and chefs who feed over 150 people breakfast and dinner each weekday. The *Washington Post* gave it an award as the best-managed nonprofit in DC. Crucial to its management prowess is Scott Schenkelberg, the program's chief executive officer. Scott says a key to his management style is an understanding that "the staff are the experts in their area of work, not me." As a supervisor, he sees his role as giving staff the resources they need to do their work, being available as a sounding board to work through issues, and making sure everyone is aligned with the greater mission of Miriam's Kitchen.

Scott's emphasis on respecting the expertise of his staff members is crucial. When congregational managers, whether they be clergy, lay staff, or elected leaders, begin to get involved in the details of an employee's work, it will often be interpreted by the staff member as a lack of respect. "I know what I am doing" is a typical reaction to an intrusive manager, church board, or committee.

Rather than interfering with daily decisions made by staff, Scott uses performance measures to have "informed conversations" with staff members, beginning with how the person's personal performance helps Miriam's Kitchen reach its organizational goals. He does not tell his staff what to do. He does not unintentionally use performance measures to stifle creativity. Instead, he uses performance measures as the basis for check-ins about how he can help solve problems. Scott also wisely refuses to use anonymous feedback in these conversations because too often, they become sources of disagreement rather than clarifying examples. (How many times has a church staff member been told, "Well, there is a member—who prefers to remain anonymous—who thinks you could do things better if you did . . ." Managing by passing along anecdotes is not only unfair. It is toxic.)

Scott's genius is that he pulls his staff into the management function. An overwhelming amount of research shows that employees are more engaged when they have significant input as to how best to do their jobs. Effective managers give great weight to the learnings of staff as they do their jobs and revise expectations accordingly. Perhaps staff discover that expectations related to a strategy are unrealistic, given the limited resources the congregation can devote to it. Perhaps they figure out a better way to accomplish what the strategy intends. Perhaps unintended consequences unfold.

The Japanese car industry competitively overwhelmed the American car industry by letting production line and other employees do their jobs while giving them significant input to shape how they do their work. Workers on the production line were empowered to lead discussions about how the cars might be assembled more quickly and with higher quality. People in charge of logistical supply chains were encouraged to suggest improvements in the process. From top to bottom (most importantly, bottom), workers became engaged as they improved their productivity with suggestions. In essence, they became managers. American car companies became competitive when they adopted the Japanese model.

We need to invite congregational staff into management. One written expectation for any worker should be to offer ideas about how to do a job better. One clear expectation of any manager should be to take staff suggestions seriously and see how they might be implemented. A skilled music director or janitor or associate pastor for pastoral care needs to be viewed as an expert. We need to treat and use them as such. If they are not an expert, then we have a different problem.

Let's dig a bit deeper into the issue of autonomy using the work of Daniel Pink, the author of the best-selling book *Drive: The Surprising Truth of What Motivates Us*. Pink lays out a lot of research revealing that the old strategy of "carrots and sticks" has lost its power with today's workers. He suggests the guiding principles for motivating today's workers are to (1) give them the autonomy to do their jobs, (2) help them master and improve the skills needed to do their jobs, and (3) align them to a sense of purpose greater than their specific tasks. Pink's focus on autonomy matches the way the staff, mostly made up of millennials, at Miriam's Kitchen is motivated by the organization's leadership.

Today's workers have a deeply felt desire for autonomy. Every manager I interviewed for this book started with a management principle rooted in autonomy: allowing their staff the freedom to do their work as the staffer deemed best. These managers supply the resources needed for the job, are willing to coach when asked to do so, and keep the entire staff focused on and aligned with the mission of the congregation/organization. But they let staff members figure out how best to do their work.

When I raise this issue in congregations, a couple of people usually respond, "But how do we know they are going to use their autonomy responsibly?" It is a fair question and needs to be discussed whenever we talk about giving our staff members increased autonomy. The answer lies in hiring staff who are responsible and creating accountability systems focused on deliverables. A deliverable might be a high-quality education class, a greater diversity of music selections in worship, or a given number of pastoral calls per month. How such deliverables are achieved is not the manager's concern, unless it involves some activity that is illegal, unethical, or harmful to the congregation. Good employees want to be held accountable. They want to produce high-quality deliverables on time. We need to give them a chance to deliver, unencumbered by boards, committees, or supervisors looking over their shoulders.

In many congregational settings, I find the pastor, rabbi, priest, or executive director is willing to give staffers the autonomy they need. What is lacking is the accountability piece. We clergy want to be liked. We do not like to scold or be scolded. As a result, we are afraid to have the difficult conversations that sometimes need to take place around the issue of accountability. Accountability is not ensured when managers stay in the face of employees. It happens when there is clarity about outcomes.

Trust is built between a manager and staffer as it becomes clear that (1) both are interested in realizing the outcome, (2) the supervisor empowers the staffer to make the changes he or she thinks are necessary to achieving the goal, and (3) the supervisor commits to helping the staffer in ways the staffer deems necessary (providing resources, including money and time, reimagining the outcome, and so forth).

Moses certainly had some accountability discussions with his people in which he laid out his and God's expectations for them. Jesus did the same with his disciples. I have always loved the job description Jesus gave his disciples when he sent them off on their own:

> Carry no purse, no bag, no sandals; and greet no one on the road. Whatever house you enter, first say, "Peace to this house!" And if anyone is there who shares in peace, your peace will rest on that person; but if not, it will return to you. Remain in the same house, eating and drinking whatever they provide, for the laborer deserves to be paid. Do not move about from house to house. Whenever you enter a town and its people welcome you, eat what is set before you; cure the sick who are there, and say to them, "The kingdom of God has come near to you." But whenever you enter a town and they do not welcome you, go out into its streets and say, "Even the dust of your town that clings to our feet, we wipe off in protest against you. Yet know this: the kingdom of God has come near." (Luke 10:4–11)

Jesus was clear about his expectations and gave the disciples some advice about how to do the work. However, he left the details to them, trusting them to do the job the way they thought best. When they returned, I am confident that there was an "accountability conversation." In other words, he asked them how they did. If they were successful, he praised them. If they struggled, he helped them understand why they struggled.

Strengths and Weaknesses

I have always maintained that I was able to stay thirty years as pastor of Western Church because we were a "match." The work that needed to be done at Western Church tapped into many of my strengths while not requiring me to do many other things at which I was less skilled. It was a perfect match.

As we manage people, we need to watch, listen to, and learn about their strengths and weaknesses. What is a staffer particularly good at? What is a person not so good at? In the areas where a staffer is not high performing, is there potential, with coaching, to raise the performance level?

We can and should coach people to improve on their weaknesses. In a radio interview, I heard the all-time great outfielder Hank Aaron say that he was born a natural hitter but not born a natural outfielder. With a goal of becoming a well-rounded performer, he spent most of his time practicing not what he was good at, hitting, but what he needed to improve, his outfield defense. As a result, for much of his career, he was not only a league-leading hitter but a Golden Glove outfielder. With coaching and practice, we should be able to improve in areas that are not our natural strengths.

Unfortunately, not all of us are Hank Aaron. Some of us will not improve much in certain areas even with the best coaching and most determined practice. Understanding the limits of coaching is as important as recognizing its possibilities. If a person doesn't improve with good coaching, we can probably assume they aren't going to improve. When we hire a staff person, we possess a basic but superficial understanding of a person's strengths. However, few people reveal their weaknesses during an employment interview. We will learn an employee's weaknesses as we observe them attempt to do tasks for which they are not well suited.

What we do at that moment will help determine whether the staffer has a productive future with the congregation. If coaching weaknesses doesn't improve performance, we need to try a different strategy. To keep the new hire, we managers will have to adjust our expectations of the employee, giving them work that plays to their strengths, as much as possible directing them away from tasks that require skills and talent they do not possess, and finding another way to get things done that we hoped they could do but that they clearly cannot accomplish. I have seen a lot of managers try to force a square peg into a round hole. I have yet to see one succeed.

An even more important question when assessing a person's performance strengths and weaknesses is, How can their strengths be enhanced and applied even further? I once managed a person who had remarkable strengths and some glaring weaknesses. As a young pastor, I focused, by coaching, on the things this person did not do well. Over time, I learned he was never going to do them well. When I switched tracks and decided to focus on this fine staff person's strengths, he became one of the highest-performing people with whom I ever worked. This, by the way, is another example of Mintzberg's thesis that management is learned more likely from experience than from a book (except this book, of course!). I learned that coaching does not always work but building on strengths may.

Daniel Pink frames the subject of building on strengths a bit differently. He talks about the importance of focusing on the mastery of skills. His thesis is simple: most employees want to be excellent at what they do. An administrative assistant wants to be known as and feel like an outstanding administrative assistant. Youth directors want to be known as outstanding at engaging youth. If a staffer does not have a desire to master the skills of their job, frankly, you do not want this employee on your staff.

Great managers understand this desire for mastery in those they manage. They talk about it explicitly: "Sharon, I love the way you want to be a fabulous youth director," or "George, I love the way you are always looking for ways to improve as our building manager." The next sentences are "Let's talk about what you need so you can be even better at your job. You tell me."

In my days as a manager, I found that a janitor might need a new piece of equipment, an administrative assistant might need an online course in Excel, and a young associate pastor might need a continuing education course on conflict management. Rather than conducting annual performance reviews, I found that ongoing discussions with staffers about how they can grow in their jobs can be much more helpful. In many instances, mastering their jobs involved not only building on their strengths but overcoming their weaknesses.

Improved mastery involves learning. While the way we learn is not a strength or weakness, it can be if managers do not pay attention to it. Each of us has a preferred style of learning. People reading this book like to learn, in part, through reading and reflection. Recognizing and utilizing the way each employee learns is a requirement for effective management.

Marcus Buckingham, a researcher focusing on performance, groups learning styles into three categories: analyzing, doing, watching.[5]

+ The analyzer learns by trying to understand every intricacy of her job and seeks out information at every opportunity.
+ The doer learns by doing the job. The more he does the job, the better he becomes at it. As he does, he learns.
+ The watcher learns by observing a job, looking at the overall task. An apprentice system is designed for people who learn by watching. When they see an expert do the job, they learn how to do it themselves.

Let's take the example of a congregation buying a new comprehensive software system. I cannot count the number of times I have arrived at a congregation to hear staff members say, "We spent a lot of money on this fancy new software, but few of us know how to use it." Why don't they? If it's a good software system, the only answer can be poor training. When I pursue how the software was introduced, I usually discover that the staff was presented with only one option for learning the new system—usually training created by the software maker. As we all know, technology people are great at creating software and less than great at explaining how it works. Having tried and failed to learn Excel by reading a book and then watching videos, my preferred learning styles, I finally resorted to Buckingham's "watcher" style. A teammate in my MBA program was a master at Excel. I sat and watched him use it, then went home and tried it myself. I was basically my teammate's apprentice.

Managers need to think about different learning styles as they attempt to help staff members develop their skills. If the training speaks to only one style, anyone who learns differently will have a hard time mastering the system. Thinking about how we will train staff should be as important as the choice of tools themselves. With janitors, I found that several learned well from a manufacturer's representative whom I brought to the church to explain a new piece of equipment. Reading the manufacturer's user manual was close to worthless. A continuing education course may work for some. It will not work for all. To learn new things, the analyzer, doer, and watcher all need a different approach to personal and professional growth.

Managing Across Generations

We have discussed different ways that staff members respond to expectations, deal with accountability, learn, and are motivated.

There is another important differentiator among staff team members: a person's generation. On many levels, not considering the generation in which a person is located is a missed opportunity by congregations. We often act as though people are generic. They are not. They are men and women, people of different races and ethnicities, from different generations, to name just a few demographic segments. At times, we need different approaches for each of these categories.

A long time ago, the business world understood the implications of what is called "demographic segmenting." They develop products for and advertise to targeted demographic groups. Watch the ads on a channel such as Lifetime, and you will almost instantly figure out whom Lifetime sees as its target demographic. Here is a clue: "Women wrote or directed 73% of Lifetime's original films from 1994–2016. Lifetime's always invested in female viewers, stories, and creators."[6] Many of the companies advertising on Lifetime are looking to sell their products to women. I have worked with congregations that use demographic segmenting as part of their growth strategies. They target young families or single people or unchurched folks. While anyone is welcome as a member of these congregations, their growth usually is among members of the demographic they are targeting.

We make the management task difficult if we do not take into account the generational segments in today's workforce. What motivates most millennials, for example, may not motivate most boomers. Today's workforce is made up of three large groups and a growing fourth one (Gen Z). In a Pew Research 2017 study, the generations in the current workforce are boomers (25 percent), Gen Xers (33 percent), millennials (35 percent), and Gen Zers and members of the silent generation (7 percent).[7] The business magazine *Inc.* reports that by 2020, millennials were forecast to constitute 50 percent of the US workforce and by 2045, 75 percent of the global workforce.[8] The *Inc.* article predicts that the domination of the workforce by millennials will result in (1) increased use of technology, (2) reliance on collaboration to accomplish organizational goals, and (3) an expectation of flexibility in all aspects of work.

Managers today need to understand the differences in generational communication preferences, lifestyle priorities, and approaches to careers. To attract younger staff members, are congregations prepared to work in the more collaborative model preferred by many millennials and Gen Zers rather than a top-down mode? Are they willing to be more flexible in the way their staff does its work and the strong boundaries many millennials insist upon to protect their private lives? Are they prepared to invest in the technology that millennials find as crucial as earlier generations found landlines and Xerox machines?

Each of us has preferences for how work should be done. Some of those preferences are, understandably, rooted in the experiences of our generation. Team discussions about the preferences of each team member will help us understand why team members do what they do in the same way that the Myers-Briggs Type Indicator helps us understand why an introverted team member, for example, has a different style from an extroverted one.

A *Wall Street Journal* column on managing different generations summarizes generations' shifting expectations for the workplace: "Baby Boomers, born between 1946 and 1964, are competitive and think workers should pay their dues. . . . Gen Xers, born between 1965 and 1977, are more likely to be skeptical and independent-minded. Gen Ys—also known as Millennials—were born in 1978 or later and like teamwork, feedback, and technology."[9] (The guide doesn't mention Gen Z and their preferences.)

One discussion that teams need to have regards communications preferences. High-performing teams regularly have agreements about the types of communications they will use—text, email, and so forth—as well as the time frame in which one can expect a reply. While younger generations are not the only ones who like text messaging, it is rare to find a boomer sending hundreds of texts per week, while it is not abnormal with Gen Z. Indeed, one study found "7 in 10 millennials and the younger Gen Z prefer to communicate digitally—mostly by text message—than in person."[10] It is easy to contact most boomers by email but usually not so easy to reach a millennial in that same way. Whether preferences turn out to be generationally based or not, discussing communication personal choices at team meetings has become a best practice.

A generational tendency coming up in many conversations is the unwillingness of younger generations to engage in the endless arguments some boomers seem to welcome or, at a minimum, tolerate. Boomers are a contentious generation. It is not a coincidence that polarization has increased in the United States as boomers have aged. Boomers (born between 1946 and 1964) started arguing about Vietnam in the late 1960s and have just changed the subject every few years. I have this amusing fantasy of nursing homes becoming highly contentious places in the decades ahead! Conflict is inevitable. Endless arguments over the same subject matter do not have to be. If we want to keep young staffers in our congregations, we need to create environments where conflict is dealt with and resolved in a healthy, respectful manner.

Dozens of pastors have told me about millennials who left their churches without expressing any hint of dissatisfaction. They did not complain about things. They just left. I have read articles from the business world reporting similar experiences. Younger employees are less likely than their older colleagues to come in and complain to their boss or coworkers about this or that. They just get another job and are suddenly gone. If these anecdotes and articles are true, and I sense they are, managers need to pay close attention to the level and intensity of conflict on a staff team or within a congregation. If they do not, excellent younger staff members may leave abruptly because they seek a less contentious work environment. I found it essential to check in with newer younger members on our staff team about ongoing conflicts within the staff team or with particularly contentious members. It was not pastoral care. It was team care.

Some in the younger generations talk about these issues in terms of emotional safety in the workplace. Harvard Business School professor Amy Edmondson, a leading scholar in this area, "has shown it's a critical factor for understanding phenomena such as employee voice, teamwork, and team and organizational learning. Feeling emotionally safe means employees feel able to speak up and communicate openly. They aren't held back by the fear that by voicing their views, they're making themselves vulnerable to criticism."[11]

Jennifer Deal, a senior research scientist at the Center for Creative Leadership in Greensboro, North Carolina, and coauthor of *What Millennials Want from Work: How to Maximize Engagement in Today's Workforce*, has a nuanced approach to the subject of generational differences in the workplace. Recognizing that there are differences not just between generations but within generations, Deal encourages us to recognize the importance of a person's life stage in shaping their attitudes and behavior. Older people, in general, want to be respected and appreciated for what they have learned in a long lifetime. Younger staff members typically will want to be "heard" by the congregations and senior clergy where they serve. Too often they can be dismissed as not seasoned enough. Both of these desires are typical of a certain point in life. Every generation feels them.

Deal and others help us understand that while much has been written and discussed around the watercooler about generational clashes, people are still people. Regardless of their generation, staff members who do not feel valued will be upset. Likewise, staff members who are praised will respond positively. While we need to be keenly aware of generational tendencies, we are always wise to focus on each worker as an individual. Managers need to ask themselves, What approaches will inspire each worker to higher levels of productivity and result in greater personal satisfaction with their performance? What practices will allow workers to protect their private lives from work? How can we get the resources our teams need to excel? How can our team create dependable, healthy communication?

Successful managers are primarily concerned with outcomes, but to get the desired outcomes, they pay close attention to a broad array of "people issues." A manager who gets everything else correct in a management puzzle but mishandles the "people" piece will never finish the puzzle.

Annual Performance Reviews

I have touched on annual performance reviews several times in passing. Let me address the topic directly: I am not a fan of annual performance reviews. Many major corporations (Microsoft, IBM, Deloitte, Accenture, to name a few) have done away with annual performance reviews. Why? In a *Harvard Business Review* article, human resources experts Peter Cappelli and Anna Tavis explain, "The biggest limitation of annual reviews—and, we have observed, the main reason more and more companies are dropping them—is this: With their heavy emphasis on financial rewards and punishments and their end-of-year structure, they hold people accountable for past behavior at the expense of improving current performance and grooming talent for the future, both of which are critical for organizations' long-term survival. In contrast, regular conversations about performance and development change the focus to building the workforce your organization needs to be competitive both today and years from now."[12]

I love Cappelli's and Tavis's take. As managers, we are concerned with improving future behavior, and a focus on past behavior almost always ends up sounding like scolding. An ongoing emphasis on helping employees develop their skills is far more likely to succeed than rewarding or punishing workers for past efforts.

UCLA business school professor Samuel Culbert has written a great deal on the shortcomings of annual performance reviews.[13] As one example of why Culbert's work needs to be taken seriously, I serve on the board of directors of a large organization that employs several thousand people. Recently, we were presented with the performance reviews of our staff. About 95 percent of the people got a positive performance review. While the organization does great work, we are not operating anywhere near 95 percent peak efficiency. Positive individual reviews do not necessarily translate into organizations or congregations that achieve their goals.

Purpose—Again

It is impossible to overstate the importance of linking all the people in a congregation—members, volunteers, and staff—to the stated purpose of a congregation. It is the great unifier. If everyone is working toward the same purpose, it is like a crew rowing in sync down a river. The power is amazing.

Congregations should have an easy time motivating staff and volunteers alike because their purpose is rooted in God's purpose for the creation. And yet how many times is the work of a staff person, including the head of staff, linked explicitly and directly to a congregation's transcendent purpose? In my experience, the answer is "too few." As a result, the sense of purpose of a congregational staffer can get lost in the details and nitty-gritty work of ministry day after day after day. The tyranny of Monday morning overwhelms the greater purpose of our work. Talented managers in congregations constantly reconnect staffers, in biblical and theological language, to the way in which their work is contributing to God's work in the world.

Of course, unfair salaries, too heavy a workload, or other resolvable issues can destroy morale. But in an otherwise fair and healthy work environment, linking each person's work to the greater work of the congregation will show results, sometimes almost immediate results. If a manager is giving staffers autonomy, helping them master their craft, and reminding them of the higher purpose of their work, the staff should be highly motivated, causing them to work in more effective and productive ways.

Marcus Buckingham, an expert on performance and motivation, discusses the importance of things that galvanize us to perform better. He proposes that each of us has unique things that cause us to be more motivated, perform better.[14] For some, the time of day may be a productivity factor. Some of us are more productive in the morning than the afternoon. If our work is aligned with our best time of day, we will be more productive. For another person, the key to more fruitful performance might be independence. The more independence a person is given, the more productive some people become.

All of that being said, according to research, Buckingham says the single most important factor to energize workers is recognition.[15] When we are given praise and recognition within our organization, we push ourselves to higher levels of performance. The power of praise. Sadly, it is an underappreciated motivator in too many congregations.

What ignites higher levels of performance with each member of your congregation's staff team? Perhaps as important, what seems to put a damper on each person's performance? Understanding what unleashes the incredibly unique and personal qualities of each staff member is crucial for a manager who seeks to maximize performance and build a happy, healthy, productive team. When it comes to motivation, a well-known saying has a lot of truth: the best bosses are the ones who do not have to do much bossing. Or, in my version, the best bosses are motivators.

Managing people is at the heart of a manager's job. Do it well and we have a much better chance of everything else falling into place. Do it poorly and we almost guarantee a mess.

QUESTIONS

1. What are your basic management principles?
2. What is most important to you when managing people?
3. When managing people, how do you help improve the performance of the overall congregational system?
4. What are your top priorities when you are hiring a staff member?
5. What is your biggest challenge and opportunity when managing a multigenerational staff and congregation?

2

Managing Information, Resources, Workflow, and Culture

In addition to managing people, managers also must oversee information, resources, workflow, and a congregation's culture. Obviously, all these elements of an organization involve people in one way or another. However, they require specific enough management expertise to generate a lot of research and articles. In this chapter, I have chosen to break them out for more in-depth discussion.

Information Management

We tend to think managers are incredibly detailed oriented. They may be, at times. However, outstanding managers seek a broad information base that contains both specific and general material. Effective managers are magnets for any type of information that will help them better understand the congregation they manage. They will seek information within the system (from staff, members, and visitors) as well as from outside it (from their best contractors, such as plumbers, roofers, and electricians; managers in other congregations; literature on management; and more). The more managers know about the congregation they serve and the resources, or lack therein, of the larger community in which it is located, the more effectively they can frame any one decision within its larger context.

The larger the context, the more likely a manager will understand the issue. A friend of mine took his car to two different mechanics trying to get a water/coolant leak fixed. Both mechanics focused on the radiator and changed various parts, but the leak persisted. Finally, my friend took the car to the dealership. They looked at the problem from its largest frame: "Let's start with the engine and work toward smaller parts like the radiator." Sure enough, the engine block had a tiny crack, which was causing it to overheat. They said, "Buy a used engine or buy a new car; your choice." Problem solved, albeit expensively. When we understand management from its broadest context and then zoom in on specific issues, we are more likely to get things right.

Given the importance of broad knowledge of an organization, its parts, and even the external system in which a congregation is located, outstanding managers are always on the lookout for new information. They are rarely content with conventional wisdom about this or that. They learn from experience and from the advice of other managers which sources of expertise are trustworthy and which are not. Have you ever bought something from someone who was supposedly an expert only to have the product be disappointing? Did you go back to that "expert"? We learn whom and what to trust from our experiences and those of others.

Interestingly, research shows that most top managers get information and find "the facts" orally. They do not get it from various forms of media (books, journals, newspapers, websites, and the like), although they do not totally ignore such sources. In congregations, good managers gather information by having regular discussions with staff, members, contractors, and others.

They will talk to just about anybody who has something to add to their knowledge base. The more experienced a manager becomes, the better the manager is at filtering out bad information and identifying helpful information. For example, after contacting a number of roofers to fix the sanctuary roof, a seasoned manager told me he was not sure who would be the best. He decided to use a time-proven managerial tactic: ask a tradesperson who has done great work for you who the best other tradespeople are. Plumbers work next to electricians, carpenters, and roofers. This manager asked his regular plumber who was the best of the three roofers he had interviewed. The plumber did not hesitate: "Hire Ace Roofing. I have worked with them on several jobs, and they do top-notch work." Experts, whether they be quality plumbers or accountants, tend to know other experts.

Although the intention of an information-seeking manager is not to become the nerve center of the congregation, the person often becomes just that. In fact, one can figure out who is doing the actual management in a congregation by observation. In a church I served as an associate pastor, I was regularly amused to see members go to the senior pastor to seek resolution of a management issue. The pastor would listen attentively and assure the member that he would get the problem solved. After the member left, the senior pastor went to the secretary and said, "How would we get this problem resolved?" She always made sure the problem was resolved. And, of course, people would say the senior pastor got the problem solved. This is not a criticism of the senior pastor. On the contrary, he knew exactly who was managing many aspects of the congregation's life, and he knew it was not him! Within months of arriving at that church, I recognized who was doing the management there and always went to the secretary when I needed something managed. Identify the information hub in a congregation, and you have usually identified the place where the manager sits.

The importance of gathering information for management casts a new light on all the phone calls, text messages, email, video chats and meetings, and casual conversations we have. These are the methods by which managers gather information in the twenty-first century. Too often I hear clergy complain that they are devoting too much time to phone calls, email, and the like. They are only a waste of time if they do not help us collect vital information that can be used now or sometime in the future as we make management decisions. Clearly, information gathering must lead to action; otherwise, it is meaningless. A manager must utilize information to mobilize the right people and resources to resolve problems or advance the mission of the congregation.

When even our informal conversations (virtual or face-to-face) are understood as information gathering, they gain a new relevance to our performance as managers. Everyone I interviewed for this book said that they have a new appreciation for this type of information gathering, since working from home has greatly reduced the number of informal conversations people are having with coworkers. The lack of information gathered in casual conversations reveals how important they are to anyone managing the staff and life of a congregation.

Most transformative strategies do not come from formal strategic-planning processes per se. They come from conversations in which we gather information that leads to strategic insights that, in turn, are fed into a strategic-planning process. As we talk with people, we also begin to consider new strategies to help implement a strategic plan. Talking with a software vendor, for example, we learn of a new program that could be used as a strategy to enhance a particular area in our ministry. The origins of this type of deductive, organic congregational change start with everyday information-gathering conversations.

Of course, gathering information is not an end unto itself. Information is meant to be shared. In the twentieth century, some managers tended to hoard information to hoard power and control. Great managers today and in the past have used information to empower those they manage. Sharing what we know with the right people has become a central task for today's managers, and the importance of information sharing is most easily observed in teams. There are no secrets in teams, no proprietary information. Team members share information with each other with the hope that it will spark creativity and productivity. Effective managers know that sharing information with the people they supervise has the same positive impact.

Fortunately, technology makes sharing information easier than it has ever been. Cloud storage of files has become an indispensable tool for managers. Documents are placed on the cloud so all team members can read everything that might be relevant to their tasks. Lists of resources can also be placed on the cloud.

For example, in the area of religious education, I can imagine a cloud document that has links to purchase supplies teachers and students might need. There would also be an up-to-date budget for religious education with line items for supplies. Teachers could see with a few clicks how much money they have left to spend on supplies. The curriculum would also be placed on the cloud, where it can be downloaded easily.

Password-protected pastoral care information can also be effectively stored and accessed by approved persons. It can also be shared, improving staff efficiency if staff post appropriate notes on all pastoral care encounters with members. Think about the crucial role notes play in our medical care systems. When nurses leave patients, the first thing they do is go to a computer station and enter whatever happened in their interactions. As these notes accumulate, they become a lifesaving resource for the medical staff in later shifts. The same thing happens in congregations where staff are expected to detail pastoral care in a way that can be shared with other staff who have pastoral care responsibilities.

I remember my frustration at finding out that another staff member had visited the hospital minutes before I arrived. In today's world, I should be able to go to the cloud on my mobile phone to track staff visits to a member in the hospital.

As a final, more mundane example, members of a congregation's building maintenance team should be able to access cloud documents such as budgets, invoices for work done, project timelines, and so forth prior to meeting. This will avoid having to spend most of a meeting going over information as a group that could have been reviewed earlier individually. Questions such as, "Was the roof finished and what was the final cost?" should be answered by going to the cloud to see if there is an invoice showing the work was completed.

Resources

For two reasons, I am not going to spend a lot of time on managing buildings. First, it is not a major issue in virtual management. Second, I have devoted a large portion of a previous book titled *The Business of the Church* to this topic.[1] Many other books and articles deal with the topic of managing physical resources. However, one resource problem comes up chronically in my consulting work. Too many congregations continue to have poor financial management systems. The result: money is either illegally or incompetently handled. In the day and age of software systems such as QuickBooks, this really is inexcusable.

The more eyes on finances, the less likely a problem will develop. Financial software such as QuickBooks or other comparable programs allows for multiple authorized people to view financial data. Please note, I wrote "view" the financial data. We do not want to give a lot of people permission to change the data! But it is easy to grant access to a password-protected file that cannot be edited.

With excellent software, financial resources become totally transparent. Staff members working from home or in the office can see the exact year-to-date status of the line items for which they have responsibility. This resolves a chronic and legitimate complaint I hear from staff members and laity alike: "I always have to ask the treasurer (or business manager) to find out how much I have spent."

Money is one of the key resources staff members and teams possess. Not allowing them to monitor their own accounts is simply inexcusable. The music director, not the treasurer or business manager, oversees the music budget; the youth director, the youth ministry budget; and so forth. Congregations need to give those who manage financial resources access to the information they need.

Managing the Workflow

Whether we are managing people, finances, or maintenance and cleaning of buildings, a key managerial function is making sure things happen in a timely and efficient manner. Leaders figure out where the train is going. Managers make sure the train runs on time and reaches the destination.

The hectic demands on a manager make this work challenging. While constantly answering emails and texts, intervening when something is not working, and regularly meeting with staff members are at the heart of managing, they can result in a manager not realizing the train has not even left the station. Effective managers have specific strategies to stay on top of their workflow. Do an internet search for "managing workflow," and you will see hundreds of pages advertising workflow software programs. If nothing else, the long list tells us (1) staying focused on managing workflow is difficult and (2) lots of managers are buying software for their companies and organizations to help them get the work done. However, software is not as important as the personal approach one uses to get work done. Students of management agree that everyone must figure out how to do that. Best practices depend on our personality as well as on that of the organizational culture in which we work. What works for one person may not work for another; what works in one culture may not work in another. But every manager needs a strategy to get work done in a timely manner.

In the past, managerial approaches to outcomes were very linear. Using the train analogy, managers thought there were a destination and a straight path to that destination. The limits of a linear approach are obvious. What happens if there is an unexpected obstacle? How many times have we heard a manager say, "The whole project went off the tracks"? As important, what happens if there is an unexpected opportunity worth exploring, an opportunity that may send us in a new, unforeseen direction? In the twenty-first century, building a railroad may not be the most efficient way to move from point A to point B.

I find promising the latest thinking for managing workflow that promotes "agility." Agile project management has a nonlinear approach to outcomes. The process leading to the outcome is flexible, allowing for discoveries along the way and discouraging workers from seeing obstacles as a sign of failure. In the early 1970s, I worked as a meatpacker for several years at Oscar Mayer. Industrial engineers designed the workflow of each employee in the plant. Based on our experience as the production line workers in the middle of the workflow, every one of us knew things that would have made the workflow more efficient. An agile approach to management would have encouraged us to make suggestions based on our discoveries as we worked day after day and implemented them where management deemed appropriate. Oscar Mayer was not agile enough to survive the twentieth century, ultimately being sold to a bigger company.

Agility enables organizations to learn as we work and incorporate that learning into next steps. Managers in such environments do not try to say exactly what step three will be until steps one and two are completed or well on their way. We can lay out possibilities for step three but should not be wedded to them. Managers who use the agile style of management talk about iterations. A process begins with an action intending to lead to an ultimate outcome, analyzes each penultimate outcome, makes necessary adjustments, and then tries another iteration. The creation of this book is the result of agile management. I write, my editor makes suggested changes, I incorporate the suggestions, and the editor reviews and sometimes makes more suggestions; at some point, we have a finished product. The book goes through several iterations in this very agile process.

If we use an agile process in a congregation, the focus will be on outcomes. How we get to the final product is the result of ongoing conversations among a staff person and senior clergy or team working on the project. In such a system, managers need to trust those doing the work. The manager's role is not to obsess over a preestablished checklist of milestones. That is a linear approach to management. The manager makes sure the team is moving in the right direction, ensuring they have the needed resources, helping them troubleshoot if help is requested, and negotiating with them if the final outcome has to be changed, given what has been learned while working on the project. How we get to the final outcome and changes we make along the way as we learn from unexpected developments are a staff person's or team's job, with the support of managers.

I have had several consulting assignments with Bishop Karen Oliveto, who leads the Mountain Sky Conference of the United Methodist Church. Covering a huge territory from the southern border of Colorado to the Canadian border, the bishop has always said, "John, we need to design an agile approach to our ministry. Given the changing conditions in our congregations, denomination, the region, and our nation, we cannot afford an inelastic approach to planning and implementation." It is not easy to make an ecclesiastical body supple. However, by making her judicatory leaner and faster reacting, the bishop is well on her way.

If the agile approach sounds like one in which autonomy, mastery, and purpose are elevated, you are correct. It is an approach for the twenty-first-century worker and congregation.

Performance

Religious congregations are, more times than not, underperforming. What performance data do I use to support such a statement? Declining membership numbers in most religious groups in the United States is a significant, albeit lagging, indicator. The declining influence of US religious groups is probably a more damning indicator. In March 2020, the Pew Research Center determined, "Most U.S. Christians perceive their religion as losing influence in America, and many go so far as to say that there is tension between their beliefs and the mainstream culture."[2] If we are not underperforming, the other option is that our core message (religious beliefs and practices) is not one that meets the spiritual needs of our neighbors. I do not think any of us wants to accept that possibility. We certainly would own that the messenger is not worthy of the message. But question the validity of a message of salvation, grace, love, justice, and so much more? I think not. Ruling out an ineffective message, we are left to conclude that the messengers are underperforming in delivering the message.

While Pew and other groups have some interesting research on why organized religion is declining in the United States, most of my evidence about low performance has been collected in the course of my consulting work. When I suggest to congregations that they are underperformers, I have yet to hear, "No, that is just not true!" Members and staff alike agree that performance is not a stated or lived high priority, and specific realities in congregational life such as declining participation in congregational programs and increasing difficulty in recruiting volunteers reveal that this is the case. An example of how performance is not valued in congregations relates to salaries. While salary levels are not the only or, perhaps, even the most important indicator of performance, they should be related to performance. If everyone gets the same percentage salary increase, we are saying that either (1) we do not link salary and performance (a position one can legitimately make but to what, then, do we link performance?) or (2) everyone is performing at the same level. I know of few staff teams where performance is equal.

When I raise the issue of salary increases, I usually am told, "We don't want to alienate one staff member from another by rewarding them unequally." But what is the message to the staff person who has created a high-performing ministry, one in which participation has increased dramatically over the past year, when she gets the same percentage salary increase as a staff person who barely puts in forty hours a week to produce a program that is struggling? Granted, a program can struggle for reasons other than staff performance. But managers need to figure out why it struggles. If it is not performance, what is it? If it is performance, why are we tolerating low performance? If we do not think some staff people are asking questions about their salary versus the salaries of other staff members and the relationship of pay to performance, we are not being realistic. Staff members know who is and who is not contributing to the team's goal of achieving the congregation's purpose. Team morale will inevitably be eroded if the congregation's managers do not see what staff members see.

The failure of congregations to even think about linking salary to performance is striking. While this failure can be demoralizing to high-performing staff, it is not the key to increasing the performance of a staff team. There is a growing body of evidence that salary is not what motivates most people once a person is being paid a reasonable wage. A recent study looked at 120 years of research on the relationship between salary and job satisfaction with a data set of more than fifteen thousand individuals. The researchers concluded, "The results indicate that the association between salary and job satisfaction is very weak.... There is less than 2% overlap between pay and job satisfaction levels."[3] This study and others like it affirm that we are wise to look for nonsalary methods of motivation, such as the three factors Pink identified that we discussed earlier: autonomy, mastery, and purpose. And let us not forget the simplest and single most effective form of motivation: praise.

To increase performance levels in congregations, leaders first need to communicate that performance is a priority by identifying clear, measurable, attainable, desired outcomes. When it comes to attainability, I would set the performance measure a bit on the low side. I'd rather have measures that teams and their members can attain so they build confidence in themselves and the system of performance measures. The managers then need to allow staff members to do the job as they know best, provide the resources they need to master the job, and communicate the importance of the purpose of their work. When outcomes are expected and connected to proven motivational management strategies, performance will rise. Effective managers will praise them when they do well!

To create high performance, Bishop Oliveto focuses on outcomes/deliverables. She designs a workload that a staff person can reasonably do in forty hours. Deliverables are designed in collaboration with the staffers. When staff members have input into what is being measured for performance purposes and how, they are more likely to view them as reasonable. If staffers produce their required deliverables, the bishop does not really care if they do it in thirty hours. This seems to me to be an eminently reasonable approach to managing employees virtually as well. It focuses on team and organizational performance and on realizing their goals, not on how outcomes are achieved or how long it takes to achieve them.

We need to decouple the performance discussion from staff members' and managers' (senior clergy and personnel committees) inevitable fear that someone will get fired, angry, or chastened in some way when deliverables are not up to expectations or delivered late. I'm grateful that congregations do not like to fire people. But we cannot let the fear of a momentary conflict over job and team performance push aside the very reasonable expectation that a congregation be a high performer. If outcomes are not achieved, we do not jump to firing or criticizing staff members. Instead, conversations need to focus on why the outcome was not achieved. Maybe the original goal was a bad one, and no one could have done it. Maybe the proper resources were not applied to the task. And, yes, maybe the team or a team member did not perform well. Even the last option is not cause for firing someone. It is cause for a conversation within a staff team or between a manager and a staffer with the intention of improving performance. The conversation does not focus on who is to blame for us not hitting performance measures. A more productive conversation begins, "OK, that did not work. What do we do now?" If we stay focused on our purpose, conversations around performance will be about improving performance to realize a purpose. We will try to understand, not assign blame for, failed efforts.

If a staff person refuses to make the changes needed to become a contributing member of the team, it is important to document the failure using best practices for human resource management, as found in the article "How to Create Bulletproof Documentation."[4] However, in most cases, we will not have to get to this step if we follow the method I have been discussing. What we should fear is not that we will have to fire someone but that we will run from our responsibilities as managers to help employees improve their performance and be happy.

If your congregation does not openly expect high performance from staff members and volunteers alike, a conversation about your culture regarding performance needs to take place. I think the conversation starts with theology. Does God have no expectations of us? Do our sacred Scriptures not lay out expectations about our performance? If God and Scripture have expectations for us, what expectations should we have for ourselves and those with whom we work? By not discussing performance, we are selling our staff short. They deserve to feel as though they are high-performing, skilled, successful employees.

If your congregation does not want to link performance to pay (again, a legitimate option), then to what other systems of approval do you link performance? A worker's personal sense of responsibility? A desire not to let down the team? A desire to remain part of the team? There are many options. But if there is no systemic expectation for quality performance, then do not expect everyone on your staff to be a high performer.

I think most of us want to be evaluated. I am probably a bit extreme; I actually hope and expect there will be a final judgment on my life. Why? I want to know what God thinks about how I performed! I think most staff members and church volunteers would like to know the same about how they are doing right now, while there is still time to improve.

Culture

Managers come into an organizational culture and must work with and learn it. Transformative managers understand the need to develop an organizational culture so it matches the needs of today's workers as well as those served. Edgar Schein, professor emeritus at the MIT Sloan School of Management, is my favorite scholar for understanding organizational culture.[5]

Schein believes culture appears in an organization in three distinct ways: artifacts, espoused values, and shared basic assumptions. Artifacts are things and practices very visible to the eye. If a culture values informality, one would expect to see artifacts such as employees dressed informally, an open office, or generative staff meetings. Espoused values are big ideas that are overcommunicated to employees and the public. At Southwest Airlines, the founder used to interrupt strategic discussions with three words: "low-cost airline." He was reminding, albeit rudely, his employees that every idea in the discussion had to come back to retaining the espoused value of Southwest as a low-cost airline.

In his work with organizations, Schein found shared basic assumptions the most difficult to unearth. Sometimes he would discover them when he noticed behaviors that did not seem to match the organization's artifacts or espoused values. An example would be a congregation whose mission statement declares it to be externally focused on the world. In practice, however, the work of the entire staff is focused inward on the welfare of the members. The controlling shared basic assumption, in such a congregation, is not the espoused value (external focus) but a shared, unspoken assumption (we better keep our members happy).

Managers will become very frustrated if they do not understand the three layers of a congregation's culture. If a new manager is redirecting staff to work externally in keeping with an espoused value, a long-tenured staff member might respond with unarticulated resistance rooted in a shared basic assumption that the mission of the congregation should be internally focused. I have observed this in congregations too many times to count. Another example is congregations that espouse the value "We welcome all." But what happens when a right-wing person sits down in a pew in a progressive congregation? In churches I have served, the right-winger was not always warmly welcomed.

What does a manager do when basic assumptions and espoused values clash? The manager can (1) continue to try to accomplish something that goes contrary to the congregation's shared basic assumptions or (2) help the congregation's leaders understand the need to clarify its values and assumptions. The first option will typically fail. The latter will result in either aligned espoused values and basic assumptions or an agreement that the basic assumption rules.

From my interviews with clergy during the pandemic, I heard that culture is even more challenging to understand and manage virtually than it is when everyone works in the same physical space. As a result, managers with staff working from home will need to be even more attentive than ever to the culture of their organizations. During the pandemic, what were the cultural artifacts that marked the virtual landscape? Did the congregation's espoused values change or remain the same? Did being virtual shake any of the basic shared assumptions to the core?

QUESTIONS

1. What are the artifacts, espoused values, and shared basic assumptions of your congregation? Would most members be able to name them? Do they need to be changed?
2. What is your congregation's attitude toward performance? What is your attitude? Are you comfortable with conflict over performance? If not, what needs to change to increase your comfort level?
3. Are you the management and information hub of your congregation? If not, who is? If not, are you fine with someone else playing this key management role?

3

Staff Teams in a Virtual World

As much as the world changes, most of it stays the same. Great managers understand this reality. It is especially important today when we hear dozens of times a day, "Nothing will ever be the same." Nonsense. We still need to pay the rent/mortgage, maintain our family relationships, preserve our health / deal with health problems, and so forth. The "new normal" has much more in common with the "old normal" than media commentators would have us believe.

For religious congregations to think "nothing will ever be the same" is particularly nonsense. In congregations, we deal with things that simply don't change, such as life cycle events (birth, graduations, weddings, death); supporting our members as they succeed/fail in their vocations, relationships, and avocations; the need to address pressing social justice issues; and so much more. When I was a pastor, I loved to look at the books that had been owned by my father, grandfather, and great-grandfather, all of whom were pastors, and consider what they would say on any given Sunday. I always decided that they would have said something not much different from what I preached. They used different vocabulary and illustrations. But the message was the same—God loves us, forgives us, walks with us, demands that we live justly.

As a head of staff, I was blessed to work with a seminary intern one year. Like most of us when we are in seminary, Eddie was filled with ideas about changing the church for the better. One day he came to my office and said, "John, we really need to change the order of worship. It is not the order my professors taught us to use. It is not contemporary enough." I asked Eddie to look on my bookshelf at a 1920s worship bulletin from our congregation. He did and said, "It is basically the same as today." I responded, "Right. And it is not our job to change it. If the people find the order of worship unfulfilling, they will let us know in a hurry and we'll change it. Until then, it meets their needs and stays the same. It is their worship service, not ours." While the number of people in worship significantly increased over my thirty-year tenure at Western Church, the order of worship was pretty much the same. We did not use male terminology when talking about God, had LGBTQ persons helping lead worship, used music from around the world in different languages, and did many more things that were not happening when I arrived at Western Church in 1983. But what I call the "acts of worship" were basically the same: calling people to worship and to confession, listening to / reading Scripture, hearing a sermon, singing hymns, bringing offerings, and the like.

As we consider the challenges and opportunities of virtually managing the staff and life of a congregation, we will remember and, at times, restate the things we covered in chapter 1. They will not change, because most of what we do as managers does not change. The fundamental things great managers do when working with people nonvirtually are the same when working virtually. We take into account the various ways to motivate people, work within the restraints of budgets and facilities, build upon and improve the congregational culture, and move the congregation toward its strategic goals.

Where Are We Headed regarding Our Workplaces?

It is always difficult to predict major societal trends. Some experts say we are seeing a revolution in work comparable to the Industrial Revolution. More and more people are choosing to work from home (I will use this term to cover all remote work). During the pandemic, the number of people working from home rose to 70 percent in May 2020 before falling to 53 percent in mid-July. The *Wall Street Journal* reports, "Even that is significantly higher than the 43% of workers who reported working from home at least part time in 2016, the last time Gallup asked Americans about their work-from-home habits."[1]

Perhaps more telling is a survey regarding the postpandemic period. Again according to the *Wall Street Journal*, "A survey of corporate leaders conducted by Gartner on June 5 [2020] found that in the future, 82% plan to allow remote working at least some of the time; 47% said they intend to allow full-time remote work going forward. A recent Microsoft survey of managers yielded the same result: 82% said they will have more flexible work-from-home policies after the pandemic."[2] Recent articles on remote work report dramatic drops in rent in places such as New York and San Francisco as people inform landlords they are not renewing their leases, preferring instead to work remotely from more affordable locations.

Based on my interviews with numerous clergy and two nonprofit executive directors, I believe that as we move into the future, congregations will have a hybrid model of work options for their staff. It is called "hybrid" because it will include staffers spending time working in congregational offices as well as working significant hours from home. In addition, some workers, mostly part-time, will choose to work entirely from home even though they will have the option of coming to the office.

Based on some of the problems clergy reported as they operated in a total work-from-home model during the pandemic, I
think a hybrid model of some work from home and some work
on-site at the congregation will smooth out some of the current
communication difficulties about which I heard from clergy during the early months of the pandemic. The biggest problem created by staff members suddenly working from home seemed to
be the absence of the casual, informal communication that takes
place in congregation offices. Even ten to twenty hours per week
on-site will create the formal and informal communication that
is so helpful to a smoothly performing staff team.

Teams and Individuals

Staff teams should be at the heart of the ministry of most congregations, even smaller ones. As I am fond of saying, we talk a
lot about congregational staff teams, but they rarely function as
teams. Instead, these "teams" are more likely to be a group of
individuals functioning not unlike the ways church staff members have functioned since the middle of the twentieth century.
The staff gathers to go over the congregation's calendar and hear
reports from each other about the work they are doing individually. The key word: *individually*. There is little talk of the staff
team's goals and strategies, little attention to aligning the team's
work to the congregation's overall mission, little evaluation of the
performance of the team or team members. In short, there are
few practices of twenty-first-century teams.

I love the definition of *team* from Katzenbach and Smith:
"A team is a small number of people with complementary skills
who are committed to a common purpose, set of performance
goals, and approach for which they hold themselves mutually
accountable."[3] Does your staff team match that definition? If
yes, congratulations, because you are an exception on your way

to being exceptional. If the answer is no, do not despair. You can build a cohesive, high-performing team.

What would a team staff meeting look like if the meeting were focused on achieving specific strategies, staying aligned with the congregation's mission, and evaluating its performance? Going into the meeting, the team would have a clear purpose with shared goals and strategies. Team members would be clear about who is doing what and how each person contributes to achieving team goals. Specific team members would apply their expertise to strategies requiring their skills, but they would do so with the help of other team members. Accomplishments would be viewed as team accomplishments, not individual or silo accomplishments. The staff meeting itself would focus on progress toward the team goals and strategies, obstacles being encountered, how the team can work together to remove them, which team member has the best skill sets to handle a specific challenge or opportunity, whether the team needs additional resources for its work, and where the team is struggling and why. The infamous staff review of the calendar? As I will discuss later, with proper software, it can be done online. It should only be discussed if there are specific problems.

The task of managing teams has some important nuanced differences from the task of managing individuals, however. Teams, in theory, should mostly be self-managing. Therefore, the entire team, as a team, should be engaged in the practices that mark excellent management. The team, as a whole, is responsible for maintaining clarity of purpose, having good communications, and assessing the need to move in a new direction to achieve its goals. Yes, the head of staff is a team's leader. But team members, not the team leader, hold one another accountable for whether and how the work gets done. Teams, not the team leader, decide how to divide up the work to accomplish their team's purpose. If a team member does not or cannot accomplish their task, the team, not just the team leader, discusses and resolves the problem. Each team member has specific tasks to accomplish, but the work of the team as a whole is greater than the sum of the individual tasks.

The head of staff or team leader becomes a coach, facilitator, and resource acquirer and deals with the external realities (congregational leaders and members, finances, and the like) that can help or impede the team from reaching its goals. In my interviews, I was impressed that every clergyperson and executive director saw themselves as a team leader. In my opinion, this is the way every head of staff or executive director should see themselves. "Team leader" is a less hierarchical approach to management and more in tune with the times than titles such as "head of staff" or "senior pastor/rabbi." I will share the thoughts of these outstanding team leaders, as well as insights from scholars and managers in the business world about managing teams in a virtual/working-from-home environment. I will spend less but some time on managing individuals virtually.

For those who serve small congregations with only a few employees, the idea of a staff team remains relevant. When I arrived at Western Church in 1983, our staff team was typical of many small churches. As pastor, I was the only full-time employee. Nonetheless, I was part of a talented, committed staff team consisting of a part-time janitor, part-time music director, and volunteer secretary/treasurer. Over the years, the team added many full-time members as the congregation grew in size, but the principles of being and managing a team remained similar.

Of course, a very large congregation has its own unique management challenges and opportunities in addition to those found in smaller congregations. An abundance of research shows that the optimum size of a team does not exceed seven. When their staff grows very large, it is not unusual for the team leader to create a smaller team of about seven key individuals who, in effect, become the senior management team. This team might, for example, include several programmatic staffers as well as the financial, communications, and lead administrative staffers. There will probably also be communications, building maintenance, administrative, financial, and programmatic teams, each with their own team leader.

Clarity of Purpose

In chapter 1, I discussed the crucial role of purpose. With a team operating in a virtual or hybrid mode, team communications become more challenging and retaining clarity of purpose more important. Just about everything done virtually has the potential to be more difficult than when it is done with the entire team physically in one location. For example, with virtual teams, everyone is in their own workspace. Because we do not see our teammates as often, we have fewer casual conversations with them about life and our work—what is working, what is not. We do not sit in the same conference room to problem brainstorm and solve. The key elements of virtual teamwork happen as we sit by ourselves, in our own space, and in front of a monitor and talk with teammates. While we are discovering how to use the videoconferencing tool effectively, it is hard to argue that it is better than the dynamics that take place as people interact formally and informally in a workspace. That being said, the benefits of working from home that appeal to some will force employers to use virtual tools more often.

Distanced from one another, team members can easily lose track of the bigger picture. As a result, teams need to spend time each meeting intentionally bringing each member's work into focus through the lens of purpose. Surely this is a key role for the team leader. As individuals talk, the leader constantly needs to connect the dots so the big picture takes shape. However, team members can contribute to this picture. As this happens, the physical distance between the members is replaced by the closeness created by a shared sense of purpose.

One senior pastor said that he starts every meeting by stating the congregation's mission and key goals. While this may feel like overcommunication to some, he says that it focuses everyone, including himself, on the bigger picture before they delve into the details of their work together.

The Covenantal Agreement

The best way to deal with things that can become problematic, such as lack of communication and some teammates not performing, is to have strong, clear, covenantal team agreements. As Laura Cunningham, senior pastor at Western Church in DC, said to me, "We are having to redraw boundaries." With more working from home, certainly boundaries between work and personal life can easily get muddied. Anything that can get confused and be misinterpreted when a team is together on-site can become even more problematic when everyone is working from separate locations. A simple misunderstanding that can be straightened out by walking down the hall requires more effort to resolve. In a virtual work setting, resolving conflict requires a phone or video-conference call. It is easy to think, "I'll schedule that call if things get worse," just to avoid yet another hour in front of the monitor.

Yael Zofi, author of five books on virtual teams, has an excellent, lengthy list of issues teams should explore as they create a covenant with each other about their team life.[4] While I recommend reading the book to get the entire list, here are a few of the ones I deem most important:[5]

- How often do we communicate? Set a date and time for regular meetings. Decide on issues about which we want to be informed by one another in between

meetings. I am hearing about team leaders assuming
team members did not want to be bothered with
a particular piece of information and then finding
out team members wanted the information. At the
beginning, as part of the covenanting discussion, team
members need to decide what people want to know,
when they want to know it, and who decides.

+ What is the team's etiquette for videoconferencing?
  Many teams do not allow members to shut off their
  video unless there is a compelling reason. (The team
  should discuss what a compelling reason might be.)
  Many teams mandate that each person use their own
  camera rather than a number of team members in a
  room using one camera. A Methodist conference with
  which I worked learned that having all the central
  office staff on one camera in a conference room was
  alienating to participants who were not in the office.
  They now have all the central office staff go to their
  own workspaces and enter the videoconference
  separately. This puts everyone on the same footing.
  Some teams even discuss whether it is allowable to
  eat while on a videoconference call. I have heard about
  teams mandating that, to speed up meetings, audio not
  be muted, thus eliminating the irritating delay when
  people search for the icon to unmute themselves.

+ Are there agendas for team meetings? If yes, who
  creates them, and when are they distributed?

+ How much time before a meeting will key documents
  be uploaded to a shared cloud space so people have
  adequate time to review them?

+ Can team members have meetings without the entire
  team present and, if so, under what conditions?

+ Is there a time limit to team meetings?

+ Can a person read and answer emails and texts while in a virtual meeting? For many groups, this would not be allowed in a face-to-face meeting.
+ How do we hold one another accountable for performance or violations of the team covenant?

A tremendous amount has been written on team covenants. Before setting up a team discussion on them, it would be wise to circulate links to a few articles to provide some background before the team has this crucial conversation. A simple Google search on "team covenants" provides an abundance of rich resources.

As the Hebrew people traveled toward their destination, God felt the need to give them the Ten Commandments to order their behavior on the journey. Teams embarking on a journey to some clear goal need their own guiding covenantal agreement.

Trust and Communication

At the heart of all teamwork and every effective management relationship is healthy communication. Trust, the sinew that holds teams together, is built on honest, reliable communications. Creating and maintaining excellent communication is challenging even when everyone is working in the same building at approximately the same hours. How does one generate and keep open, honest communication within a team when much of the communicating is done virtually? This is a major challenge of our times.

Only one group of people can determine how a team can best communicate: the team itself. When creating its covenant, it is the first topic of conversation for a team. It is a conversation that can never end. As a team works together, it will discover where there is good and poor communication and discuss how to protect the good while eliminating the poor communications. The prior example about a Methodist conference central office staff is a case in point. They did not realize, at first, that having some people in a conference room, whispering to each other or laughing about things that were not audible to those on the call, was a problem. When they identified the problem, they changed their behavior to make sure communication was solid. It is the team leader's role to make sure communication remains a high-priority discussion topic month after month. However, if any team member feels there are problems with communication, it is their responsibility to bring it up for a team discussion.

To develop great team communication, the best path is to focus on several key areas, some of which we have discussed:

+ Purpose: What is the team supposed to do? Communicate it some more. The research is unanimous that clarity of purpose is the single most important factor for a team's success. Surely the purpose will be communicated to team members by whoever creates the team. However, it needs to be discussed at length in team meetings to ensure each team member is on board. Purpose cannot be overcommunicated.
+ Expectations: Who is supposed to do what and by when? When expectations are clear, performance rises, which in turn builds trust and minimizes conflict. "Nobody told me to do that" or "Nobody told me it had to be done by tomorrow" conversations will be reduced greatly. Team discussions to clarify who is doing what and when things are supposed to be completed are at the heart of healthy team communication.
+ In-progress commentary: How does the team talk about giving one another feedback? One of the great strengths of teams is the opportunity for teammates to give each other feedback. Members of high-performance teams report to each other regularly about how they are

doing on their specific piece of their team's larger work. If they are having problems, they can solicit the advice of teammates. If the suggestions are constructive, trust will be built, and individual and team performance will move to higher levels.

+ Keeping it helpful: How do we keep feedback constructive? Communication around in-progress problems can be tricky. It can easily devolve into personal criticism rather than constructive comments designed to help the entire team accomplish its goals. The team leader and the team itself have to communicate often and well about problems they are encountering and solutions they have discovered.

+ Shared information: How is information shared? Unless there is a compelling reason not to do so, all team members should have access to all the information related to their team's work. Today, this is typically done using cloud storage of key files and documents. The team's cloud storage can contain everything from flowcharts to financial documents to progress reports from individual members. Generally, in today's almost paranoid culture, failure to share information will be viewed with suspicion. "Why can't we see that? What are they hiding?" Once these toxic questions are asked, communications are broken. Only transparency will repair them. Appropriately copying team members on emails is another way to keep a team on the same page.

+ Failure: What do we do when we fail? How a team communicates around failure—whether the whole team or a particular team member is to blame—will determine the team's ability to overcome failure and find new ways to realize their purpose. In science, a failed experiment is viewed as a positive development.

A failure shuts off one path of inquiry, pointing the researchers in another, hopefully more positive, direction.

In congregations, too often failure is viewed as, well, failure. Blame, guilt, and denial follow failure in many congregations. Teams should be able to communicate about failures. Why did it/they/I fail? Is the failure one we can work around, or do we need to junk the project and do something else to realize our purpose? Does one team member need to step up and say, "This is my fault. If I had done my job better, the team wouldn't have failed"? If so, do the teammates agree in a supportive way or attempt to view the failure more as a team failure? Until congregations develop a healthier approach to the role failure plays in God's ways, they will make life more difficult than it needs to be.

Building and Maintaining a Sense of Belonging to a Team

The fragility and strength of bonds in virtual teams is something I probed in-depth with the clergy and executive directors I interviewed. The congregational teams that existed prior to the pandemic seem to bring strength from their face-to-face connections into their new virtual state of being. Many team leaders reported that team strength started to fray as weeks of virtual work together turned into months. As problems were identified, however, they were discussed, solutions identified, and adaptations made to restore the strength of the teams.

In the beginning of the pandemic-induced transition to virtual teams, Ellen Agler, the experienced executive director of Temple Sinai in Washington, DC, told me she had a strong team built during years of face-to-face work. Agler explained it was sometimes challenging for her and the team to identify what needed to be done in a virtual setting. Despite these issues, however, since the various teams were strong prior to the pandemic, they were able to adapt and problem solve on their own. This is what great teams do! Sometimes the teams instinctively broke into smaller units to tackle specific issues. Focusing on what needed to be done, the deliverables, these teammates held one another accountable as they identified their work and found creative ways to do it. This, by the way, is exactly what Mintzberg recommends when he talks about pushing management down to the managed. When team leaders empower teams to make decisions, to manage themselves, the results can be amazing.

What key things did people do to build and maintain strong teams as they moved from a face-to-face to virtual existence? I discovered some clear, important themes as I interviewed congregational leaders across the country.

Staff Meetings

The importance of staff meetings increased as a means of maintaining team connections. The interviewees described a variety of approaches. Arlene Nehring, senior pastor of Eden United Church of Christ (UCC) in Hayward, California, has a weekly one-to-two-hour team meeting. They discuss everything from building use (the building is used mostly by several social service programs deemed "essential" by the local government) to worship planning to pastoral care. Arlene believes the weekly meetings kept the team connected and performing well. She also noted the fact that helping the poor is deemed essential by the secular government, while worship is not. With a determined smile, she commented that the prophets agree with this judgment: for example, "Do not oppress the widow, the orphan, the alien, or the poor; and do not devise evil in your hearts against one another" (Zech 7:10).

Scott Schenkelberg, CEO at Miriam's Kitchen for the Homeless in Washington, DC, said they tried weekly "watercooler" general-conversation meetings to stay connected. However, they were not deemed effective by the staff so were discarded in favor of shorter, more task-oriented meetings. Another pastor reported a similar experience. She said weekly virtual meetings lost their vitality once the novelty wore off.

Of course, boring virtual staff meetings should hardly surprise us, since staffers from time immemorial have complained about boring face-to-face staff meetings. Too often they can be a huge waste of time. As an associate pastor in the early 1980s, I served on a staff that certainly felt this way. During the meetings, each of us would report to the senior pastor and, in theory, to each other about our work. While I guess this was supposed to enable us to see how our work was interconnected, the individual reports were never linked to the larger mission of the congregation. As a result, the reports felt more like show-and-tell.

Staff meetings need to have a clear purpose. Many congregational staff teams have found weekly virtual meetings important, as they discuss pastoral care and worship and go over the calendar to make sure everyone is on the same page. Certainly, pastoral care and worship planning will engage and require input from each member of the staff. For example, I regularly got crucial pastoral care information from our music director and administrative assistant.

I recommend that congregations investigate calendaring software options that allow staff to see, in real time, what is happening and where. Good software can also allow committees and teams to book times and spaces with their smartphones, with an administrative assistant / calendar manager approving them within twenty-four hours. Such an online calendaring system will greatly reduce the amount of time at staff meetings devoted to calendars.

Peter James, senior pastor in Vienna, Virginia, decided to go with more frequent but shorter videoconference team meetings. Bishop Oliveto does the same with a fifteen-minute check-in meeting at the beginning of each day. The large staff divides into small groups for discussions. David Taylor, an international businessman, said he has felt the need for more frequent meetings to keep his team, located across the Americas, connected and high performing.

Life as a Zoom Call

The mushrooming number of videoconference calls has clearly had a deleterious impact on many people for multiple reasons. "Everything is a meeting now," said Rabbi Roos, senior rabbi at Temple Sinai. It is an insightful statement illuminating the way staff team life has been transformed by going virtual. Every single person I interviewed complained about the larger number of meetings compared to when they worked on-site. Bishop Oliveto said the increased number of meetings is so exhausting that she changed the staff's work schedule to four, ten-hour days to give people a longer weekend to recover.

Why are there so many more meetings using videoconferencing? First, it is easier to meet. With face-to-face meetings, one needs to get in a car, walk, or use mass transit to get to a meeting. With videoconferencing, one just gets in front of a camera. Second, with the time for the commute eliminated, there is, literally, more time available to meet. Typically, I would allow one hour on either side of a face-to-face meeting if I had to travel. Not having to travel frees up two hours for additional meetings.

In Louisville, Kentucky, Leigh Bond says that he is spending a lot more time on follow-up with staff and programmatic teams than in the past. He says this is directly related to the staff being predominately virtual. In the past, he could ask someone a question by walking down the hall or discussing something in the parking lot. Now he has to formalize communications by sending staff members a text or email or scheduling a conversation. The informal follow-up management that was done in the office is now requiring a lot of formal virtual time.

Laura Cunningham, senior pastor at Western Church, said she never realized how many crucial informal conversations she had during the day around management and pastoral care issues. Every pastor talked about the way they would see a staff member in the parking lot, have a quick conversation, and resolve an issue. It now requires increased intentionality to address issues, using a video call, emails, or text message exchanges.

What happened to using phone calls for management? An *Inc.* article says, "People are shunning the phone in favor of chat apps and texting, not just in the workplace, but as consumers."[6] Some avoid the phone because text messages and email give them time to think before responding. Others prefer text and email because they can attach key documents or links. Others like the "paper trail" that messaging provides.

Numerous interviewees said that many balls were dropped until they figured out that they used to pass key managerial information along in informal conversations. For example, one pastor said there was confusion about who was going to contact a home-bound person. The two pastors finally realized that they usually double-checked on home visits during passing conversations.

Many clergy expressed deep concern about the impact of so many video calls on the relational aspect of their work.

+ Bishop Oliveto said, "I worry that we are losing our humanity" because of our lack of face-to-face interaction.

+ Ed Harding, senior pastor of Prince George's
  Community Church, said, "For someone who likes to
  touch, this is painful to me as a pastor. People are dying
  without a touch or even a prayer."
+ Rabbi Roos said that intimate moments such as bar/bat
  mitzvah meetings with a young person and their family
  are now video meetings. "It isn't the same."

All three and others talked about this issue as problematic for
the maintenance of a sense of team as well as for the staff's relationships with members of their congregations. They believe this
concern will disappear somewhat as the impact of the pandemic
subsides and people are able to engage in face-to-face encounters
again. However, in teams that increasingly rely on doing some of
their work from home, teams and their leaders will need to be
very intentional with strategies to maintain "the touch."

Another major issue arising from the large number of video
calls is fatigue. While people identified different reasons for the
fatigue, everyone agreed they are exhausting. Eyestrain and back
strain from too much time in front of a monitor are common
complaints. However, one also needs to pay much closer attention
to interpersonal dynamics while on a video call. This increased
attention creates its own fatigue. Whether this will be less true as
our communication is increasingly virtual and thus more natural,
we do not know.

One or Two Teams?

Team building is affected when some members work at home
and others are on-site. Several interviewees noticed the creation
of two staff cultures—one for the virtual staff, the other for
the on-site staff. Hal Chorpenning, senior pastor of Plymouth
Congregational UCC Church in Fort Collins, Colorado, said

he has a hybrid staff, because some people work from home, while others prefer to work at church. Kris Thompson, chief executive officer of Calvary Women's Services, a social service program for homeless women in Washington, DC, described a similar phenomenon. Part of her staff needed to be at the shelter to provide direct, frontline social services. Other parts of her staff could and did work from home.

Both Hal and Kris reported that the folks who work on-site developed into a team within the larger staff team. They retained and benefited from the informal communication system that existed before the pandemic forced some staff to work from home. This caused some communication problems with staff members who were not on-site and therefore not privy to the informal communication system. Information was not shared equally across the larger staff team. Neither Kris nor Hal feared their teams would suffer greatly because of this division, believing it would end when the pandemic ends. However, it did complicate team building and communication. When teams become hybrid—one group working both on-site and at home while another group works totally on-site—will the on-site group develop its own communications that, in effect, leave out those who are sometimes working remotely?

I find the evolution of a staff team into at-home and on-site components to be important because of these communication issues that, in turn, become team culture issues. Team leaders need to develop intentional strategies to make sure the two groups (on-site and work from home) do not become two separate teams. People working on-site will have the advantage of the informal communication that is lacking in most virtual settings. It could easily develop an "insider" mentality if the people on-site feel better connected to each other than they do to their teammates working both from home and on-site. Keeping both sets of staffers communicating and working together is a primary task for staff team leaders as they manage one group of staffers working from home and on-site while another group works totally on-site.

The emergence of a two-team situation is not a totally new challenge. Many staff teams are made up of a combination of full- and part-time members. Heads of staff talk to me regularly about the challenges of keeping part-time staffers integrated as members of their team and in the communication loop. The communication issue part-time staffers face is similar to that of virtual staffers. They miss out on the crucial informal communications that take place in face-to-face settings because they are not on-site as much.

Accountability

We have all been on teams where one or more members simply did not perform. The team may have worked around the problematic individual, but doing so took energy that could have been used constructively. As bad, it took the fun out of working on the team. At the heart of high-performance teams are norms that ensure accountability. Each team needs to determine its own norms for performance. These norms will cover everything from communications to productivity to timeliness. Team members need to hold themselves and one another to the norms.

The norms lead to members working within agreed-upon boundaries but not to micromanagement. Study after study reveals that micromanagement is counterproductive with at-home workers, just as it is with on-site workers. The authors of a *Harvard Business Review* article assert, "Employers who allow employees to work remotely should grant these employees true autonomy and flexibility, rather than trying to micromanage their remote work. Our results comparing WFH (Work from Home) and WFA (Work from Anywhere) employees indicate that granting greater autonomy can actually enhance employee productivity."[7]

Even on a team, micromanagement is a problematic strategy. A team leader or member may begin to micromanage others in hopes of their getting the job done. We immunize a team from micromanagement when we focus on deliverables. If someone is delivering what is expected of them, we should not be concerned about how they did it (unless, of course, they did so in an unethical or illegal manner). We get into how someone else works only when deliverables are not produced on time or the quality is below expectations. Even then, rather than questioning a teammate's specific work practices, a better approach involves asking, "Is there anything we can do to help you get this finished on time?"

Overseeing a United Methodist conference covering a huge geographic area (from southern Colorado to the Canadian border), Bishop Oliveto finds the management challenges are exacerbated by the lack of reliable broadband and even cell phone service in some areas. When I was conducting focus groups for the conference, some individuals drove an hour or more to reach a place where they had adequate internet speed.

I asked the bishop how she holds her staff accountable in such a huge area with sometimes problematic communication systems. She responded, without hesitation, "Deliverables." For her, the issue is this: Does the person get the job done; is the desired work product delivered?

The bishop's approach matches just about everything one reads about best management practice these days, virtual or not. When teams have clearly defined deliverables, it is much easier to hold them accountable and for them to hold themselves accountable. Either the job gets done or it does not. There is not a lot of wiggle room in such a system.

A sensitive issue for staff team management involves the need for each team member to have the skills needed for work in the twenty-first century. Many congregations with which I consult are aware that they have current staff members who are not agile with computers or software. They love the staff person but not their work product, which is limited by their lack of technological skills. What to do?

The easy part is making sure we hire people who have the computer and software skills needed to be a team member in our time. If new hires have most of the skills but not all, good managers make sure they immediately get the training they need during the start-up period. The technology problem I see most often is inadequate training on the congregation's customer relationship management (CRM) system, which tracks membership data, giving, and often finances. Effective managers find out how a person learns and provides them training that matches their style.

The greater challenge is determining if a current staff member can continue on the team despite a lack of needed skills or an inability (or unwillingness) to gain them. This situation is even more challenging when the folks lacking these skills are long-term employees of the congregation. They might have become the church secretary back in the day when things were written on a typewriter rather than in a word processer, and they might have learned how to use the latter, but that has been the end of their learning.

I have seen church leaders who work in the business world become incredulous that congregations often have a difficult time releasing employees, especially longtime employees who may have lost effectiveness as technological job demands have increased. They do not understand that congregational employees usually develop a constituency within the membership. The janitor is more than a janitor. Janitors are usually beloved fixtures in congregations, whether they do a good job or not. Ironically, the businessperson demanding performance accountability may be the first to ask, "Why are we letting George go? I love George. Everyone loves George."

How do we move an ineffective but beloved staff member off the team? I wish I could tell you I have an easy answer to this dilemma. The two most common approaches I see are (1) gradually reduce the scope of the person's work to nontechnological tasks until the person leaves or retires and (2) give the person a generous buyout package to move on. Neither approach will completely assuage the staff member's friends and fans in the congregation. Both, however, are fair and deal transparently with the issues.

In his book on virtual teams, Yael Zofi writes, "Accountability is like the fuel flowing through the engine of the team. It is the essential bond that enables the team to operate successfully. Team members must have faith in their colleagues' ability to deliver. This is true for all types of teams, and even more so in the virtual world, where bonds are more fragile."[8] In managing, accountability cannot be overstressed. Congregations underachieve in large part because there is a huge lack of accountability. Do not expect high performance when there is no emphasis on performance accountability.

Conflict

In a virtual context, an area that requires significant attention is conflict. Virtual or not, conflict within a team is challenging. Conflict puts overall team dynamics and the team leader's skills to the test. Psychologist Bruce Tuckman became famous with his "forming, storming, norming, performing" paradigm for teams. In his studies, he decided that conflict over how a team operates is crucial to it performing well. In his progression, the "storm," or conflict, should lead to the creation of team norms that will clarify roles and the way the team will operate moving forward. Religious communities are infamously conflict averse—a strange fact because every religion has stories within its tradition where conflict is a catalyst for positive change. But it is what it is.

Everything I have read about conflict within virtual teams talks about how disagreements can accelerate faster than they would face-to-face. Virtual conflict moves from simmer to boil very rapidly. Certainly, most of us have seen this happen with email exchanges. Flat text (e.g., memos, emails, text messages) can mask a sender's emotions. It allows a reader to impute emotions to a sender that may not have been present. For example, a reader may sense anger flowing from a sender's words when, in fact, there was absolutely no anger present.

The same phenomenon can be at work in video calls. While video calls are certainly an improvement over the voice-only conference calls of a not-too-distant past, we still do not have the full sensory experience with teammates that we would have if we were all in the same room. We have all described someone as "bristling" in a meeting. Much of "bristling" is a sensory experience, not visual or heard. We feel the "bristle." Even in a video call, we may not pick up the full feelings or might misinterpret the feelings of our teammates.

In interviews, numerous congregational staff team leaders talked about how communication around conflict, potential or real, sometimes became a problem during the pandemic. When I interviewed people for this book, we had been in a new, virtual mode of operating for only four to six months. And yet staff team communication breakdowns were described to me as a significant problem.

As one team leader said, "When we were all in the office physically, before the pandemic, I heard or saw things that suggested the possibility of conflict. In such cases, I made a point of checking with the relevant team members to defuse a problem before it became a big problem. Working virtually, this type of communication is difficult, at best. There is no 'office' where I can pick up on things."

Another team leader talked about how her staff asked her much more often about what was happening in leadership video meetings where they were not invited participants. She sensed irritation that they were being left out. In fact, these meetings had been held prior to going virtual, but no one ever asked her about them.

What had changed from the prepandemic dynamics? When everyone was in the same building, it was easy to ask a meeting participant, "Was there anything I need to know from that meeting?" in a casual, passing conversation. However, when everyone was working from home, there was a sense that something was happening in video meetings they did not attend but that there was no way to find out if there was anything they needed to know. The team leader defused the issue before it became an actual conflict. She started taking extensive notes during the virtual leadership meetings and shared the relevant information with various staff members who didn't attend.

Finally, it is easy for people to "hide," not participate, on video-conference calls. People may hide intentionally because they haven't done their work and don't want to talk about it or because they are introverts. Lack of participation can lead to hostility from team members who are more engaged. They may decide that the members who are not participating are not carrying their share of the load. To prevent conflict from developing, the team leader on calls needs to make sure that everyone speaks and has an opportunity to express views. Asking nonparticipants if they have anything to add is a simple way to avoid people from hiding.

Bishop Oliveto oftentimes uses the mutual invitation model to get everyone participating. In this model, no one can interrupt a speaker. When speakers finish, they ask another person to speak.

People can pass if they do not want to speak. But they must invite someone else to speak next. It is a gentle way to encourage and create space for everyone to speak. I believe this method is compatible with virtual team conversations.

Some bad habits that inhibit virtual communication—such as multitasking while on a call (reading material, sending texts, etc.) or literally hiding behind a photo instead of having the video turned on—can create conflict. When setting ground rules for videoconferences, these issues need to be addressed so conflict can be avoided.

Bringing in New Team Members

Ed Harding, senior pastor of Prince George's Community Church, reminded me of the importance of establishing a well-designed process for adding new members to a staff team. He said, "I hire people because they have clear competency for the task (e.g., youth ministry, administration, music). However, what they will not have is cultural competency. They do not know the culture of our staff or our congregation. So I spend a lot of time with them in the early days making sure they understand the way our team and congregation function culturally."[9] Competency of task versus cultural competency. The distinction is brilliant. Still, if it is difficult to bring a new staff member onto a team when the team meets face-to-face, how difficult will it be to add a person to existing virtual staff? I suppose some might argue that joining a virtual team will be easier because the team bonds might not be as strong as with a face-to-face team where years of informal communication have produced strong personal ties.

I would argue that the same issue (informal communication) will make it harder for a new person joining a virtual team. New members will not have the advantage of asking a long-standing team member, over a cup of coffee or in the parking lot, "What's up with that?"—whatever "that" is. A *Harvard Business Review* article makes this point: "Based on our research—which focused on already-experienced employees—it seems best to keep newly hired employees co-located in the office with experienced peers long enough to benefit from the informal learning that happens organically in a face-to-face environment."[10]

I am working with several clients who are virtually hiring people for their staff teams. It is challenging enough hiring people when we can have multiple face-to-face encounters with candidates. The difficulty goes up significantly when we are limited to only virtual interviews and conversations. Think of how a typical process works. We read résumés, limit the number of candidates, and conduct phone or video calls. Then the finalists are brought in for face-to-face interviews, which are viewed as crucial. During the pandemic, some were forced to eliminate what many consider to be the most important step of an on-site visit. When doing interviews with no face-to-face encounters, we have reduced the opportunity to see how someone interacts with others. We have a limited or, at a minimum, a very different "feel" for a person. But hiring people virtually has been a necessity, not an option.

Going forward, many groups may continue to hire virtually because there are some advantages. For example, during the pandemic, I was hired for three jobs with virtual interviews. In one case, part of the hiring team interviewed me and recorded the interview so the rest of the team could view it later. It was a very efficient process. Obviously, there are also cost savings when a group doesn't have to fly in candidates for final interviews. It will be interesting to see what congregations do in the future, given some strong positives and negatives to a virtual hiring scenario.

How do we bring the new person onto the virtual team? I suggest that we go back to the basic strategies for making a team cohesive: practicing excellent communication, focusing on deliverables, and skillfully working through conflict.

We will need to ensure that the new person understands how and when the team communicates—for example, using text, email, video calls, and so forth and during what times of day. The team's covenantal agreements need to be explained in detail with examples of times communications worked and times they failed. In the new person's first meeting with the team, it is crucial to ask the new person to discuss issues such as communication preferences, introvert-extrovert dynamics, what makes the person happy at work, and other information that makes for strong teams.

In the first weeks and months, it will be important for team leaders and teams to support a new member as they learn how to function in a new environment. We need to make sure they feel comfortable asking questions and to be responsive when they do. As a team experiences a new person's reliability and a new person hears the team's praise for that reliability, the new person will be welcomed to the team in a new way, not just as a member but as a high-performing member. The importance of the trust created when team members come through on their assignments cannot be overstated.

In an ideal world, a new member's first experience with team conflict would involve difficulties between other team members. After a conflict is resolved, the team leader can say, "And that is how we work through conflict. We do not deny it exists or run from it. We work through it transparently and respectfully."

Finally, when bringing a new person into a team, I suggest having one team member (other than the team leader) become a mentor. This is true for virtual or on-site teams. However, with a virtual team, the mentor can also fill in some of the blanks that occur when there are no on-site informal watercooler conversations. The new person can call the mentor to ask questions about team behavior or the idiosyncrasies of other teammates or the team leader. "Why does that person always challenge me?" "Why isn't the leader more assertive?" and other such questions need to be answered in confidential sidebar conversations with a mentor.

Just as I have stressed the importance of the prehiring steps needed to hire good people, the onboarding of new team members is just as crucial. During the onboarding period, a new member is going to make some judgments about the team, teammates, and the larger organization. If the judgments are negative, they will inhibit the person's work. Ron Carucci, a consultant for Fortune 500 companies, writes, "I've found that the most effective organizations onboard new hires for the duration of their first year—their most vulnerable period—and focus on three key dimensions: the organizational, the technical, and the social. By using this integrated approach, they enable their employees to stay, and to thrive."[11] Organizational onboarding involves teaching new employees how the organization works. Technical onboarding involves making sure they are clear about what they have to do. Social onboarding pays attention to helping them feel like part of the community. An abundance of helpful literature on this topic is available with a simple internet search.

The Culture

Let's go back to Ed Harding's insight about the importance of integrating new team members into a congregation's and staff's culture. Culture is at the heart of who we are and what we do. Jennifer Howard-Grenville, a professor at Cambridge, has a fascinating article in *MIT Sloan Management Review* about the impact remote work is having on organizational culture. She says, "Some organizations are finding that long-desired changes, like decentralizing their decision-making or becoming less bureaucratic, have suddenly—and surprisingly—taken place in mere weeks."[12] Of course, the unanswered question is whether these changes will survive when many of the people working from home return to on-site work.

No doubt the same is true in congregations across the country as they have moved to virtual work. What changes will remain? What changes will disappear? Ideally, congregational leaders wonder, "What specific congregational and staff culture changes have occurred in the congregation I serve?" and "What changes should take place as a result of what we are learning from the pandemic?" Following Schein's logic and research, Howard-Grenville says identifying cultural change is best done by looking at the practices of an organization. To see the changes in a congregation and answer the questions just posed, we should look at practices that are changing.

Identifying changing practices is more challenging when people are working from home, however. Howard-Grenville says, "Culture is ultimately about the actions we take and make visible to others, and the meanings we invest in those—which is harder, but not impossible, to maintain from the kitchen table."[13] Wise congregational leaders will devote significant meeting time to strategic conversations about changing practices within the staff and congregation and the changing culture they may reflect. Has decision-making decentralized with the work of virtually operating teams becoming more important? Do we have the technology we need to do ministry in the twenty-first century? How much time should we spend working on-site, at home, and in the community? And most important, did what we learned about ourselves and our community during the pandemic mean we need to redefine our congregation's purpose?

While I am generally optimistic about the changes taking place as congregations move to a more virtual reality, the matter of culture concerns me. Congregational culture is at the heart of who we are. Yes, we have our faith commitments and beliefs. However, our practices are often rooted in something other than a belief system. For example, there was something in a racially segregated congregational culture that closed it off to any teachings in its belief system that racism is evil. So my optimism about the ability of congregations to respond to our changing time is tempered by the practices of many congregations that reflect the secular culture, not the teachings of the major faith traditions in the United States. Following Schein again, the practices are more representative of the congregation's basic assumptions than the espoused values. If we adopt virtual practices without making sure they are used to express the basic assumptions of our faith traditions, it will be the same as a superficial coat of new paint on a house whose foundation is fatally flawed.

Just as congregational culture is at the heart of its functioning, staff cultures are at the heart of how a staff performs. In many congregations, the staff culture has very low expectations about performance and encourages conformity, not creativity. In other congregations, staff cultures encourage an entrepreneurial, high-performance approach. In some congregations, the culture is dominated by governance systems designed to resist rather than initiate and support change. In other cultures, congregations have designed governance systems to empower change and increase impact. Culture matters.

The good news is that the shift to a virtual reality is forcing many congregations to ask fundamental questions about their culture and the practices it produces, questions that should have been asked decades ago. Every single clergyperson I interviewed said the pandemic is forcing their congregation to ask, "What is our purpose? Who are we? What are we supposed to be and do?" Many said a question as basic as, "Do we need a building, and if so, to what end?" is now on the table.

Howard-Grenville observes, "A time of disruption presents an opportunity to remind employees of aspects of an organization's past—founding ideals, stories, and commitments—that have shaped both its culture (how we get work done and think about our work) and are central to its identity (who we are as a company). Building up these core elements of culture can remind employees of an organization's strengths and help them navigate tough times."[14] Shouldn't staff teams be responding to the opportunities our time of disruption is presenting? Shouldn't we be asking, "What about our staff life together is essential to our performance and central to our identity—and what isn't? Where can technology improve our ability to achieve our purpose, and where might it impair it?"

As we enter a time when virtual teams will grow in importance in the life of congregations, we need to remember that not everything virtual is good or bad. Not all technology is beneficial or harmful. We need to be analytical and reflective as we become more virtual in our way of being as congregations. With the use of technology, we have an opportunity to shape and reshape congregational culture for decades to come.

QUESTIONS

1. As your team becomes more virtual, what are you doing to make sure communication is excellent?
2. Do you have a covenant or code of conduct for your team's virtual work? How well does it cover issues such as communication, timeliness, and conflict?
3. Do you have specific deliverables for each member of the staff team to accomplish the team's overall goals? How do you manage a person when the deliverable is not produced in a timely manner or the quality is not what was expected?
4. When was the last time you devoted a large block of time for the team to discuss the congregation's culture and the

team culture? If you have such a conversation, will you design it, have the team design it, use suggestions from sources expert on the subject of teams, or something else?

5. How do you bring new team members onboard a team—virtual or on-site?

4

Virtually Managing a Congregation's Program and Life

My assumption is that postpandemic, many congregations will use a hybrid of face-to-face and virtual meetings for governance and management of programs. In my interviews, people expressed a strong desire to return to the office while retaining the option of working from home. While many virtual teams can generate a strong sense of belonging over the long haul, I think becoming totally virtual during the pandemic was hard for those that previously functioned face-to-face. As Shannon Kershner, senior pastor of Fourth Presbyterian Church in Chicago, told me, "Anything that was a tad dysfunctional became full-blown dysfunctional for a time."[1] Staff members missed the social interaction and the key role it plays in making decisions. It is much easier to pop into someone's office and ask a question than it is to go back and forth with emails or texts. Others want to return to the office simply because they do not like their homes becoming their workplaces.

However, there is also a realization among congregational leaders that operating virtually has some real advantages. It is easier to call a quick meeting, meetings tend to be shorter and more efficient, and it creates more flexibility in one's day to run personal errands, to name a few. Therefore, moving forward, I see many staff teams adopting a hybrid model of operating in which staff split their time between working from home and in the office.

Managing the governance and program systems and the volunteers in them is at the heart of any successful congregation's life. Just as managing paid staff virtually has unique challenges and opportunities in comparison to managing them face-to-face, the same is true with volunteers. Having seen the ease with which a team of volunteers can meet virtually, many people will not want to spend time driving to their congregation's building to meet face-to-face. But will the staff person managing such a team be able to exert the influence that often happens in face-to-face meetings?

A virtual operational mode, which allows volunteers to be much more independent, might actually require less supervision. Talking with several pastoral nominating committees during the pandemic, I asked them how they were doing using a virtual model. They were overwhelmingly positive about the process. They said it was much easier to get together virtually both as a committee and with candidates because they did not have to use group-scheduling apps to find times convenient for everyone for a face-to-face meeting. They went face-to-face when they brought in candidates. However, they quickly reverted to virtual meetings to evaluate the candidates and finalize their decision. The committees described an operational style that was agile and self-managing.

Volunteers

Arlene Nehring is the senior pastor of Eden United Church of Christ (UCC) in Hayward, California. I love her insight that volunteers offer their time because they are looking for something rewarding to do. For most, it is a truly selfless act. Volunteers sense a need, a problem that requires resolving, or an opportunity that creates the chance to do some good and serve God. Rather than letting someone else do it or letting it go undone, they step up and offer their time, skills, passion, and often, money to meet the need.

Before I address the specifics of managing volunteers virtually, I want to acknowledge the commitment of volunteers as one of the greatest and most inspiring parts of involvement in a religious community. In Washington, DC, where I live, if religious communities stopped feeding the homeless, helping immigrants integrate into our society, working with victims of domestic violence, and carrying out so many other key social activities, the hole in the social fabric of our city would be immense. No government can afford to do what religious and other volunteers do for free.

When I first started spending time in our second hometown, San Miguel de Allende, in Mexico, the small expat community was not involved in many organized ways with the Mexican population. As the predominately American and Canadian community grew in size, a wonderful thing happened: volunteer organizations popped up to feed the hungry, work with orphans, create housing, address environmental issues, fund scholarships for poor students, and so much more. As this happened, the Mexican community not only got involved; they created their own volunteer organizations beyond those created by the expats. As a result of both Mexican and expat volunteer efforts, the environment has a group of strong advocates, poor people have access to a few more services, young people are able to go to the university level, and local women have been empowered in wonderful ways. As Nehring says, all of these volunteers are looking for ways to make a difference. Indeed, their personal reward is the felt experience that they are making a difference.

Do congregations typically view their volunteers as individuals seeking to make a difference? I'm not so sure. I know at times I viewed volunteers as people who solved my problems. When I needed another usher, an additional hand in the kitchen, or someone to fill a hole in the Sunday school teaching staff, I was grateful and relieved when a volunteer appeared. But was I trying to give them a rewarding experience? Not always. At times, my approach was more utilitarian, about me rather than the benefits for the volunteers. I do not think I am the only pastor who falls into that bad habit.

Just as it is important to be clear about the purpose of staff and each individual staff member, it is equally important to identify and name a clear purpose for each volunteer task. If that purpose is significant, helping the congregation achieve its purpose, we need to make sure volunteers see their efforts in that light. We needed ushers because they are a visitor's first contact with the congregation and therefore essential to church growth. When I let ushers know that fact, they usually shined in their performance. When I resorted, in a rush, to focusing them on activities—handing out bulletins and getting down the aisle on time to collect the offering—their performance was not as high. We make a volunteer's work rewarding when we directly connect it to broader goals that generate satisfaction. They understand that they are making a difference.

In addition to connecting volunteers to the purpose of a congregation and, ultimately, to God's work for the congregation, making sure that volunteer teams are high performing and enjoying their work has to be high on a manager's list. Zac Sturm, senior pastor of Atonement Lutheran Church in Overland Park, Kansas, told me that he leaves volunteer teams alone when they are doing well. He only gets involved if he sees hints of a team struggling to get its work done. Hovering over a team unnecessarily is a sure way to turn the experience negative. He not only wants teams to generate a product. He also wants their experience to be rewarding. To do so, he tells teams how important their work is to achieving the goals of Atonement Church as he tries to ensure that they have a positive team experience.

How many times have we heard someone say, "I'll never serve on a church committee again. It was just too frustrating. Nothing got done. All we did was complain"? (Shorthand: "It wasn't rewarding.") When volunteers give us their time, skills, and commitment, we owe it to them to make sure they will have a rewarding experience. The proven way to make sure volunteers feel positive about their contributions is to overcommunicate to them the difference they are making. The usher needs to know that welcoming visitors ties directly to the congregation's desire to grow. The person volunteering in the kitchen needs to know how a delicious meal feeds not only stomachs but a sense of belonging to a community.

Diversity and Inclusion

With this overview of some key aspects of managing volunteers, we move to specific opportunities presented when managing them virtually, most often in meetings. While we all complain about meetings, deep down, we know they are essential for accomplishing the work of a congregation. As volunteer teams meet, work is envisioned, a plan of implementation created, and ongoing supervision of implementation provided.

Virtual meetings have a huge advantage over face-to-face meetings that is not being widely discussed—namely, they allow people to participate who otherwise might not be able to do so. Many people who might feel excluded from on-site meetings can participate in ministry activities more easily if they don't have to leave home and can instead meet virtually. If meeting times and places create childcare issues, people with young children are less likely to serve on boards, committees, and teams. Many seniors do not like to drive at night, when many congregational meetings are typically held. Too many times I have heard low-income folks say, "I can't afford to miss work to attend a meeting." People with various types of disabilities may be reluctant to participate in meetings, especially if there are physical access issues such as a lack of ramps and accessible restrooms in the meeting location. Many people simply do not want to spend time driving to and from meetings, especially if they've already suffered a lengthy commute to and from work. If we are serious about being inclusive, having meetings where almost anyone can participate is crucial. For all of the people in these groups, a virtual meeting is so much easier than attending a meeting at the congregation's building.

High-functioning teams meet often but make decisions quickly. Given the ease of gathering virtually, teams can also function more effectively because members will be more willing to meet regularly to plan and assess their progress. Virtual meetings also allow groups to gather to address urgent concerns with little advance notice. Whether as a standing or spur-of-the-moment meeting, a noon weekday videoconference may allow people to join from their workplaces. Since virtual meetings tend to be shorter, even someone working two jobs may be willing and able to take a break at work, step outside, and call in to a meeting. A Saturday-morning meeting can actually be quick when one eliminates the commute to and from the congregation's facilities. If they have to drive to church, folks may balk at meeting. If the only thing involved is getting on a videoconference, though, there will likely be less resistance. I work with a nonprofit where we have learned that we function more efficiently because we now have short, drop-of-the-hat type meetings to solve this or that problem.

Both ongoing and emergency business can be conducted virtually, ensuring decisions include the contributions of members who otherwise might be unable to participate because of childcare needs, driving limitations, or time constraints. Congregations need to start touting this incredibly positive aspect of technology to enable the work of a congregation.

A caveat regarding the benefits of calling people together easily is that it can be abused. I know people who have dropped off boards because instead of one monthly meeting, they were being asked to meet more frequently for less than urgent matters. Boards, committees, and teams need to have as one of their covenants agreement about the purposes for which special meetings can be called. This allows people to opt in or out at the beginning.

Governing Boards

Even as boards resume meeting face-to-face, I believe most are going to decide to operate in a hybrid mode. Their primary meetings will be face-to-face, but emergency or other types of meetings will be held online. Examples of emergency meetings would be a major financial surprise that needs to be addressed immediately, a staff issue that cannot wait, and a building repair cost that will blow up the budget. As governing boards embrace their new hybrid existence, they will learn the strengths and weaknesses of both virtual and face-to-face meetings as well as the dynamics common to both. Strengths of virtual meetings include things like being able to meet from wherever you are located rather than driving somewhere, the fact that virtual meetings tend to be shorter and more to the point, and being able to easily hear what everyone is saying. Strengths of face-to-face meetings are related to the group bonds that develop, the ability to distribute hard copies to everyone rather than hoping they downloaded them, and a better sense of body language by participants. Weaknesses of virtual meetings are related to the inferior sense of "feel" for one another, the possibility of technical problems like voices breaking up, and eyestrain for some while watching monitors. Weaknesses of face-to-face meetings include the potential for extroverts to

	STRENGTHS	WEAKNESSES
Virtual meetings	◆ People can participate from any location. ◆ Meetings tend to be shorter and more to the point. ◆ It's easier to hear everyone in the group.	◆ Participants have more difficulty getting a feel for one another. ◆ Technical problems crop up. ◆ Group members can experience eyestrain from watching monitors.
Face-to-face meetings	◆ Group bonds develop. ◆ Hard copies of documents can be distributed. ◆ Participants can read one another's body language.	◆ Extroverts can more easily dominate. ◆ Meetings tend to last longer. ◆ Getting to and from the meeting takes time.

dominate, their tendency to last longer, and the time invested to get to the meeting.

Whether a group meets virtually or face-to-face, conducting business with a large group—say fifteen to twenty-five people—is less than optimal. The problems can increase when a large board meets virtually and are rooted in the way extroverts take over large meetings. Introverts are more inclined to speak in groups of fewer than nine. Additionally, it is challenging to have an in-depth conversation when the time is limited to, say, two hours and so many people have to be given an opportunity to talk. As a result, many congregations have downsized their governing board to twelve to fifteen members. For those that have not, now is the time. During the pandemic, I worked virtually with numerous boards of varying sizes. The smaller ones adapted to virtual meetings with relative ease. The larger ones struggled. They did not adapt, because the same group dynamic issues large boards struggle with face-to-face were present—extroverts taking over and lack of time for everyone to have a chance to speak. It is challenging for many introverts to elbow their way into a face-to-face conversation at a board meeting. Add the other inhibitors many people feel on video meetings, such as discomfort or lack of dexterity moving quickly from mute to talking, and the problems of large videoconference meetings can overwhelm some participants.

It is important to note that even organizing a smaller-sized group does not ensure introverts will be more at ease or able to express their thoughts. According to Leigh Thompson, J. Jay Gerber Professor of Dispute Resolution and Organizations, "Research indicates that in a typical six-person meeting, two people do more than 60 percent of the talking. Increase the size of the group, and the problem only gets worse."[2] To anyone who moderates meetings, that research probably sounds spot-on.

All of this is to say that creating a safe, comfortable environment for introverts to offer their thoughts requires planning under any circumstances. Fortunately, a great deal has been written about what introverts need to stay involved. As one example, Renee Cullinan writes in a *Harvard Business Review* article, "Extroverted thinkers are happy to get new information in a meeting and to start making sense of it by talking through it. But introverted thinkers make their best contributions when they've had time to process relevant data and space to choose words carefully and share thoughtful conclusions. So while the extroverted thinkers are buzzing away, the introverted thinkers are quiet, still processing the information. Extroverts often misinterpret this silence as disagreement, disengagement, or lack of subject matter expertise, and often don't make the effort to bring the introverts into the conversation."[3] In any meeting, it is important to get information, especially new information, to board members well before the meeting, giving introverts time to process it and form their thoughts.

To encourage equal participation by extroverts and introverts, Bishop Oliveto uses the breakout room feature in their videoconferencing software to create small groups (two or three individuals) during staff meetings. Justin Hale and Joseph Grenny strongly endorse the approach in an article on getting participation in a virtual meeting. They recommend not just setting up breakouts but specifically asking the small groups to discuss actionable topics. Unlike extended presentations or PowerPoint decks, the focus on action in breakouts keeps people engaged because they learn that they will regularly be asked to problem solve and make decisions. Hale and Grenny explain how the size of a group can impact the response of those present: "Research shows that a person appearing to have a heart attack on a subway is less likely to get help the more people there are on the train. Social psychologists refer to this phenomenon as diffusion of responsibility. If everyone is responsible, then no one feels responsible. Avoid this in your meeting by giving people tasks that they can actively engage in so there is nowhere to hide."[4] (Indeed, "hiding" on video calls is now a technical term. It refers to people who turn off their video to not participate. The latter, in particular, should be outlawed in the covenants teams create for their meetings.)

I have used breakout groups for strategic-planning meetings with various boards. It does not eliminate the problem Thompson describes, where a couple of people can dominate a small group. Typically, that requires a group leader to control the dominators. Small groups, however, do create a space in which introverts will feel comfortable contributing to the discussion and where all participants will be actively engaged.

As an example of a well-functioning group, let us drop in on a congregational governing board that is meeting virtually to discuss the $45,000 budget deficit that has developed through the first half of the year. If the board discusses this as a group, a small number of people will no doubt become strong, vocal advocates for various responses. Indeed, as we listen to the conversation, people perceived to be experts on finances in general, or the congregation's finances specifically, dominate. However, when the moderator directs the board to break out into small groups to discuss the problem, things change. Almost instantly, there is a much higher level of engagement. In small groups, participants remember a basic but often-ignored fact: each of us has to balance our own finances; we are all knowledgeable about the bottom line. Indeed, some of the participants are experts at personal financial management. With that understanding, the small-group participants bring their understanding of personal finance to the plight of the congregation's finances. Undaunted by the congregation's "financial experts," they quickly and firmly take control of the discussion. When the moderator brings everyone back together, ideas flow freely from the small-group discussions. Some of the experts are pleased by the increased interest in finances; some are dismayed, as they realize the new confidence of other board members to address financial issues means they are no longer in control. Once we become comfortable with the breakout group feature that exists in most videoconferencing software programs, it is easy to design discussions like this, where the group alternates between a larger group and smaller groups.

While the issues for virtual meetings are not totally dissimilar from those of face-to-face meetings, they have a unique twist to them. Clearly, leading virtual meetings involves more than sending out the link for a call. Transfer the dynamics of face-to-face large and small groups and differing extrovert-introvert preferences to a video call, and the problems can be magnified by practical challenges some experience in a virtual discussion. For example, some people feel uncomfortable seeing their own image on-screen. Or they lack the dexterity to move quickly from mute to talking or to hit the "raise hand" icon, increasing the effort required to join a discussion. The group leader or moderator needs to watch participants carefully for signs that someone wants to talk.

During the pandemic, as boards held all of their meetings virtually, I noticed people becoming considerably more comfortable with the format and growing in their ability to tackle complex issues. Organizational agility itself can increase by adopting a hybrid modality (virtual and face-to-face). Calling a face-to-face special meeting of a board is very cumbersome. I am on a board that decided we can hold special virtual meetings with less than a twenty-four-hour notice. We still need a quorum. However, we can act fast in response to events that demand our attention that day. The flexibility has been transformational. We are more informed and engaged than in the past when we had face-to-face meetings once a month. Again, it is also easy to abuse the ability to call special meetings. Groups need to make their own rules about what constitutes "special." If not, participation in the special meetings will quickly decline.

Committees and Teams

Committees and teams are two separate entities. Committees are governance-related groups formed by a governing board or bylaws. They are assigned responsibility for specific tasks such as overseeing finance or personnel. These standing groups are closely accountable to the governing body that has committed some of its authority to them.

Teams are action or task rather than governance oriented. The word *team* first appeared in the English language to describe teaming animals together to increase their productivity. A congregation might have an ushering team, a kitchen team, a feed the homeless team, an environmental justice team. Sometimes teams are formed by individuals who share a common interest or goal. Sometimes they are formed by a staff member or the governing body. While accountable to the governing board, they are very much entrepreneurial in that they have the freedom to do their task as they deem best. Their work is approved or assigned by the authorizing committee or board. However, how they perform the task is totally their responsibility. They usually report to a board or sponsoring committee when they are finished or need additional resources to accomplish their work.

Increasingly, congregations are moving to an organizational structure with fewer committees and more teams. In large part, this reflects generational preferences. While the boomers were comfortable with committees, younger generations have a strong preference for the action orientation of teams. They have grown up functioning in teams in sports and the classroom and now in the workplace. Typically, they do not want to sit around in a committee meeting deciding what work needs to be done or trying to recruit people to do it. They want to do the work with a few teammates.

Unfortunately, some congregations have simply changed the names of their committees to teams without changing how the groups function. If it looks and acts like a committee, it is a committee, not a team! In other words, if a group talks about what work to do but wants someone else to do it, you have the essence of most committees. If you have a group that sees work that needs to be done and only wants permission to do it, you have the beginnings of a team. Fortunately, many congregations are eliminating many of their standing committees and embracing the use of entrepreneurial teams to accomplish their mission.

The virtual management of employees and many of the tools we are discussing in this book have been used by teams in the business community for many years. Business corporations have few inhibitions when it comes to doing their work with teams. David and Beth Taylor, accomplished businesspeople, have worked for global corporations. Beth, now retired, worked on an international team where she never met her teammates face-to-face. And yet, says Beth, she had close working relationships with her teammates. All their collaborations were done with email or telephone conversations. Perhaps the biggest issue was scheduling meetings across time zones, since Beth lived in the United States, while her teammates were in the Philippines and India. While Beth's team was limited to phone conversations and email, they were a highly successful software-development team. When it came to accountability, the team used clear performance measures. When someone missed a deadline, Beth would get on the phone and talk with them to negotiate a new due date or suggest solutions to whatever problems caused the delay.

Using mostly video communications, David manages a staff located outside the United States in the Americas. He says that managing his teams virtually is not much different from face-to-face. He uses the best practices for management per se, laid out in the first chapter of this book. For example, he said that when managing face-to-face, he would regularly pull aside team members to see how they were doing. Now, managing virtually, he sets appointments to do the same thing with a videoconferencing or phone connection. He pays a lot of attention to his virtual team culture, just as he did when he had his team in the same building.

As with governing boards, virtual tools give congregational committees and teams the ability to be very agile. Instead of having to gather people in a physical space, it is very easy to set up a quick video call to discuss a problem that pops up or explore an opportunity that needs to be addressed immediately. Such meetings are especially useful when they are short, as this encourages people to contribute efficiently rather than participate in dreaded meetings that drag on and on. While there can still be bad meetings, my interviewees uniformly reported that meetings had become shorter and more efficient.

Team meetings should be focused on a team's specific tasks. Trying to get everyone together on an ushering team for a face-to-face meeting, for example, can cause a lot of frustrating scheduling work. Getting the same group together virtually or face-to-face should be easy using online scheduling software such as Doodle. I am confident that moving forward, teams will meet more regularly than in the past because it is easier with virtual tools not only to meet but to set up meetings.

Toward the end of my time at Western Church, I got a taste of how software can help teams operate better by adding virtual components. Our Sunday school teachers decided to use online software sold by Basecamp to share information. Basecamp advertises itself as "the premier project management + internal communication tool for remote WorkFromHome teams worldwide."[5] Before Basecamp was introduced at Western Church, teachers had to have special face-to-face meetings to share information about their lesson plans, scheduling, and issues related to students. With Basecamp, it was all done using the teachers' tool of choice: smartphones, tablets, laptops, or desktops. After a class, the teacher would inform her coteacher teammates what she accomplished on Sunday, when she taught. She would also mention if there were any problems with students or interactions with parents. This allowed the following week's teacher to step into the classroom informed and up to speed. In contrast to email, this built up a one-click source of information about what was happening in the class. A teacher could scroll back to see what happened weeks ago. Teachers would also use Basecamp to reschedule teaching duties when an emergency arose. For example, if a teacher had a sick child at home, he would send a message to his teammates saying, "Can anybody cover tomorrow? I cannot make it. I'll cover for you on your next Sunday." Again, not only does the communication take place, but it can be easily referenced at any time in the future.

Basecamp was introduced to our Sunday school by Amy DeLouise, a documentary filmmaker. From her business use of Basecamp, she learned how much time the software saved her production team as they managed complex filming and production schedules all on the same website. It had a similar transformative impact on our teachers. As word spread about the way teaching teams were using it, we had less trouble recruiting teachers. Their teaching schedules, the downloadable curriculum, background information about students or parents, the ability to swap teaching days, chats about things learned while teaching, archives for key information, and so much more were all available in one online location. Instead of searching around the house for the curriculum the teacher put down somewhere last month or trying to find the church directory and then calling a teacher to find out what happened last week, the teachers went to the Basecamp site, logged in, and had what they needed. If that is not an incentive to go virtual, I do not know what is!

My guess is that selection of team members in a hybrid world will be even more crucial than it has been for totally face-to-face teams. One criterion will be the ability and willingness to meet virtually. If a team is hybrid, each team member needs to have a reliable internet connection and a device with a good camera and microphone. Hybrid teammates will also need to understand how to or be trained to (1) make a team covenant regarding communication and accountability, (2) identify conflict and what to do with it, and (3) differentiate when face-to-face meetings rather than virtual ones are necessary—for example, to bring all the

Sunday school teachers together to thank them and have some social time together.

Even formal committees will benefit by doing more of their work virtually. A finance committee, entrusted with fiduciary responsibility for the financial affairs of a congregation, needs accurate timely information. In prepandemic times, this usually meant receiving an email with current financial reports as attachments. The committee then met face-to-face to discuss the reports.

Utilizing the tools of a virtual world, the reports can be posted in the cloud, where any committee member can locate and review them at his or her leisure. As a result, the treasurer won't be getting emails from committee members saying, "I can't find that email. Can you send it again?" Finance committee members may also be enabled to review (but not edit) the operating budget, examining the line-item detail using software such as QuickBooks. While the committee may want to meet quarterly for a face-to-face review and discussion, it can meet monthly with a videoconference to ask questions of the relevant staff or treasurer. Such calls can be recorded so that anyone missing the call can view it at a later time.

If it was a face-to-face meeting and you missed a meeting, you were out of luck. You got somebody's verbal recollection of what happened or minutes to read. The recordings are a major upgrade to those two options. I recently interviewed for a consulting job with three members of a nine-member team. They recorded the interview so the others could view it at their leisure. I think that will become a best practice for many teams.

The finance committee could also have videoconference calls with governing board members or staff who have questions about the financial reports. I have always been concerned that the discussion of financial reports consumes so much of a governing board's time. While finances are important, conversations about how to grow the congregation, deepen the spiritual lives of congregants, serve the community better, or create religious education opportunities are more important. A constant complaint I hear about congregational board meetings is this: "All we talk about are finances, the building, and sometimes personnel." Prior to a board meeting, board members can be given a link to where financial reports are located on the cloud. There they can easily compare older reports to current ones. If board members have questions, some of the finance committee members, the business manager, or the treasurer can hold a virtual question-and-answer session at a time separate from the board meeting itself.

A major issue for every church member is time. For many twenty-first-century Americans, time has become more valuable than money. Congregations have learned this fact in many ways. For example, they are willing to pay someone rather than find a volunteer to sit in the nursery or hire a landscaping service rather than having members volunteer to do the work. Getting people to volunteer to be on teams and committees has become a universal challenge for congregational leaders. Making team and committee meetings easier to attend and quicker and having information more accessible will make recruitment easier. It has the effect of making the organization leaner. The less energy going into the governance and operation of a ministry, the more energy available for ministry to members and the community.

A final warning: just because it is easier to meet virtually does not mean we need to meet. I am hearing an endless stream of complaints about the way virtual meetings are multiplying out of control. We need to listen carefully to folks as we increase the virtual aspects of our ministries. If I know anything, I know they will tell us if we are abusing them with too many meetings.

Program Creation and Management

In most congregations, programs in areas such as education, fellowship, or mission are generated by a staffer, committee, or team. In the pre-start-up phase, new programs get massaged by some group of individuals with knowledge and interest in the area. The start-up itself is assigned to a staffer or volunteer, with supervision delegated to a staffer, committee, or team. How does all of this work in a hybrid world?

Working with a small denomination in the middle of the pandemic, I was asked by the leadership to run a process to generate a lot of strategies for meeting specific goals in a strategic plan created by the governing board. Meeting in person was impossible. As a result, we created brainstorming teams to meet using videoconferences. The results were phenomenal. Each team thought up highly creative strategies. What I loved about the process was that we took advantage of the virtual possibilities for people to meet. Instead of having a group of people in one geographic region meet face-to-face, we were able to gather people around the country with deep knowledge in the various ministry areas. One group decided to invite some experts from outside the denomination to be part of the brainstorming. The outside experts were able to contribute information about best practices from their much larger perspective.

Think about how this might work in a congregation. Typically, a group of members and staffers would get together to brainstorm about new programming. In this traditional approach of using a congregation's staff and members to generate ideas, the thinking is limited to that relatively small group. Worse, it is limited to the pool of knowledge within the congregation. The group may have little or no knowledge of key issues that need to be addressed. What would happen if the invitees were expanded to include outsiders? By expanding the participants to people outside the congregation who have expertise in the area of education or religious education, for example, the conversation changes from a strictly internal conversation, limited by the knowledge of the members and staff of the congregation, to one that engages the best minds in the community or even the nation. Or, rather than having a middle-class suburban congregation discuss strategies for addressing poverty in the bubble of their affluent suburb, why not bring in, via videoconference, community grassroots people who work with the poor? In the past, it would have been challenging to get experts or community leaders to agree to participate. They are busy people; why meet with this particular congregation? However, with videoconferencing, invitees only have to agree to give thirty to sixty minutes of their time while never leaving their office or home.

Or what about a conversation to develop strategies to combat systemic racism? Instead of having members and staff discuss it in a vacuum, what about inviting to a videoconference the president of the local NAACP chapter, leaders and members of the Black Lives Matter movement, and the local chief of police? Getting such people to drive to the congregation would be challenging. Getting all of them to commit to meeting at the same time would probably be impossible. But having them join for an hour on a videoconference? That is likely doable.

Another option enabled by technology is videoconference focus groups. I use them all the time in my consulting work to get feedback from congregational members, staff, and others about important issues. When considering a programmatic idea of some sort, why not hold a few focus groups with members of your congregation (and perhaps community members) to get feedback before investing time and money in a project?

When I first started consulting, we had to invite people to physical locations for focus groups. Videoconferencing makes it much easier for people to participate. The input from focus groups is far more creative, in my experience, than surveys. As one research firm notes, "While survey research has limitations on the number and type of questions asked, focus-group queries are open-ended and interactive, so that an almost unlimited number of variables can be explored. Because of its open and exploratory nature, focus-group research can also stimulate discussion about ideas not anticipated, or topics not included in the discussion guide used by the moderator."[6] Many times, I have emerged from focus groups with ideas far more important than and different from the idea I was exploring when I organized the focus group.

Designing congregational programs is, in many ways, the easy part. Implementing and managing programs are the bigger challenges for many congregations, usually due to a lack of clear deliverables. A key to successful management is measuring the timeliness and quality of the deliverables, which will be just as important, perhaps more important, when managing congregational life in a hybrid modality. Teams that meet regularly in a virtual mode do not have the luxuries of lengthy face-to-face meetings where things can be thrashed out or informal water-cooler conversations to resolve small problems. Therefore, from the very beginning, team members need to have extremely clear expectations about what they are supposed to deliver and when it needs to be delivered. Ultimately, I think most lengthy face-to-face meetings will disappear. They are too time-consuming and can be filled with unhelpful drama. As mentioned earlier in this book, time today is more valuable than money for many. People have grown intolerant of long meetings. They show their intolerance by not showing up regularly or losing focus while present. In this hybrid period, however, meeting virtually more often will help us understand the importance of deliverables: what we are supposed to do, and how long we have to do it.

In my interviews with clergy for this book, I have been told repeatedly that it is harder to virtually manage program work than staff teams. Why? Many congregations have some written expectations for their staff. However, too many congregations do not have clear deliverables for their programs. They don't have concrete answers to key questions: What difference will our Sunday school make in the lives of the students and teachers? What are we trying to accomplish in our music ministry in addition to producing beautiful music? What does a sustainable financial future look like? Going back to the old management adage, we cannot manage what we cannot measure.

Congregational managers are not as experienced managing virtually as managing face-to-face, but I anticipate that, over time, they will grow more comfortable with the nuances of virtual management. Using a hybrid style of management will smooth out some of the discomfort some clergy feel with virtual management by giving them some face time with those involved in programs. That being said, in the hybrid world, every manager should be asking those managed, "Is there a way we can manage our programs more effectively by using technology?" As Laura Cunningham at Western Church told me, "In the future, every aspect of ministry will have a digital component."

QUESTIONS

1. Define an "effective board meeting," and then ask, Did your governing board's effectiveness increase when it was meeting virtually during the pandemic? If so, how? If not, why?

2. As teams and committees met virtually during the pandemic, did you hear positive, negative, or no comments about that transition?

3. Do you anticipate teams, committees, and boards continuing to rely heavily on virtual rather than

face-to-face meetings? If so, why? If not, do you intend
to encourage groups to meet virtually, given the increased
diversity of participants virtual meetings can generate?

4. Is your congregation using software tools such as
Basecamp and QuickBooks online to facilitate a more
virtual approach to ensuring good communication and
shared information across the congregational system? If so,
what has improved? If not, what has prevented the shift to
virtual life?

5. Has your congregation brought nonmembers into
the congregation system using software tools such as
videoconferencing to give advice or offer perspective on
programs the congregation is considering starting? If
so, what has been the result? If not, what have been the
barriers?

5

Life at Home and in the Workplace in a Virtual World

Not all is well at home. While some people enjoy working from home, many others do not. Joseph Polzer, professor at the Harvard Business School, frames the issue perfectly: "Are we working from home or living at work or both?"[1] As I interviewed people about their experiences of going virtual during the pandemic, a number of congregations reported a hybrid approach to work, with some staff going into the office, in states where it was permissible, while others stayed home. Postpandemic, most congregations will offer some type of hybrid arrangement where staff can work in the office or at home.

What is not clear, from my interviews, is whether congregations are considering the burgeoning research on the impact on work productivity from working at home. Perhaps more important, are congregations examining the impact increased work at home will have on their staffers and their families? For example, working from home can create the false illusion to others in the home that a person is available for family time when, in fact, they are not because they are hard at work. Working from home also eliminates the face-to-face interaction at the office that might be an important element of work for some people. As people were forced to work from home during the pandemic, scholars were studying the impact it had on everything from productivity to teamwork to increased rates of depression to divorce rates to childcare. My interviews also revealed that few congregations are anticipating the physical changes in the design and safety of offices that some staff will demand as a result of the pandemic experience.

Congregational governing boards are most effective when they focus on policies that will guide and empower their ministries. Most congregations have human resource policies about salaries and benefits, conflict resolution or mediation, and sexual misconduct and harassment. Moving forward, I predict that congregations will need to develop policies about

- supporting staff and volunteers who do some or all of their work from home,
- ensuring a healthy, safe workplace, and
- guaranteeing that the congregation's needs are met through high productivity by staff working from home.

While we are learning as we go on this topic, we know enough about working from home to create policies that will nurture healthy work–personal life balance and protect the physical health of our staff. This chapter focuses on what we can learn about the experience of working from home from the business community, where it is not a new phenomenon, as well as my interviews with congregational leaders. Projections about the future rely on the same sources.

Segmentors and Integrators

In the past, many of us who study management have observed that some staff members like to work at home, while others prefer

their offices, and numerous theories are put forth about why this
is so. Given the research done over the past fifteen years or so,
the reasons people prefer their offices are clearer. Two key dif-
ferentiators between the groups are covered by the widely used
terms *segmentors* and *integrators*. While these terms have broader
implications for working people, beyond whether they are working at home or in the office, some of which we will discuss, they
are directly relevant to a work-from-home or office discussion.

Segmentors like to create clear boundaries between their
work and personal lives. These individuals do not want calls
from home while at work; they do not want calls from work
while at home. They try to create and live in two distinct worlds.
Management scholar Nancy Rothbard writes, "A strong segmentor
aims to finish up work calls while at work, even if it means staying a bit later, and might only participate in a parent story hour
during a lunch break."[2] To use a concept *Seinfeld*'s George Costanza
made famous, segmentors don't want their worlds colliding.[3]

In sharp contrast, integrators are comfortable dealing with
all of their worlds at the same time. They can sit at work and
make doctor appointments and balance their personal checkbook
while on a work-related videoconference. They can sit at home
and have long discussions with work colleagues about pressing
business questions. They can watch their child play sports while
doing important business by phone or texting from the sidelines.

On a staff, the differences between segmentors and integrators can create conflict and misunderstanding. The integrator may
get irritated that a segmentor teammate does not respond to text
messages early in the morning or late at night. The segmentor will
get irritated that she is expected to answer the text messages. The
integrator starts to wonder, "Does Sarah care about his work?"
The segmentor thinks, "Peter is compulsive about work."

Segmentors and integrators also may have different views
of commuting, which is generally viewed as a necessary evil.

(One study estimated that the pandemic saved American workers eighty-nine million hours per week.)[4] During the pandemic, we learned some new things about the role commutes play in the lives of some people. Some segmentors realized that the commute can be a helpful part of their day, not a waste of time. The *Wall Street Journal* and other newspapers published articles during the pandemic revealing that for some people (segmentors, in particular), the commute serves as a crucial bridge between their neatly divided worlds. One commuter talked about using his time on the train to work as a crucial transition where he transformed himself from his family persona to his work persona. Hopefully, the transformation is not as extreme as Dr. Jekyll and Mr. Hyde, but it was major, nonetheless. The person who got off the train near his office was not the person who got off the train at the stop near his home. For such individuals, the transition time is crucial to maintaining a separation between the work and home worlds.

I once worked with a person who asked me if she needed to keep her office door open, as I regularly did. I responded, "Of course not." Her sigh of relief was audible. I learned part of the reason for her relief when we did the Myers-Briggs Type Indicator and she turned out to be a strong introvert. Introverts are usually more comfortable working in a space where they don't have to interact constantly with others. Looking back, I now realize that another part of her relief was rooted in her segmentor personality type. Our staff knew little about her personal life not because she was an introvert but because she did not want the personal and professional to merge. Indeed, she was not even that keen on sharing her work world with others. The open door represented opening her work world to the public.

Working from home is extremely challenging for segmentors. If they are able to create a separate space at home dedicated solely to work, they get some relief. However, if their family room is both their office and a place where the family interacts, it is a problem. If a spouse or children or pets roam through their workspace, it is a problem. If a lawn service is creating noise outside while they are on a videoconference, it is a problem. Having to work all the time at home, during the pandemic, was a huge problem for segmentors.

During the pandemic, numerous articles in my local paper, the *Washington Post*, were published about couples who decided to move from apartments to houses. A home that was adequate for their personal lives was not adequate when they were forced, by a lack of space, to become integrators. They wanted to set up areas for their work that were segmented from their personal lives. Another article described a single person who became uncomfortable with his efficiency apartment because he could never get away from his work.

As the pandemic eased, it was a fairly safe bet that many of the congregational staffers who were eager to get back to the office were segmentors. The need for camaraderie and the desire for collective brainstorming with colleagues were not the only reasons for their return. What they yearned for was to separate work and home. For most segmentors, returning to the office was a source of relief from the work–personal life integration taking place at home.

As the pandemic eased, most integrators would have enjoyed returning to some mix of working at home, the office, and elsewhere. The pandemic caused some organizations to offer the option of working totally from home. The people accepting that offer will include some integrators but also those segmentors who are comfortable and able to create a totally separate space and time for their work from home. Indeed, for some segmentors who can create a home office, not having to deal with the interruptions inherent in office life would be ideal.

Just as a staff team needs to have an explicit conversation about the Myers-Briggs preferences of each team member, so a team needs to understand who is a segmentor, integrator, or some of both. Integrators and segmentors need to respect each other's lifestyles by creating covenants about who can be contacted when and how outside the office. For example, during what time frame each day can teammates expect responses to their texts, emails, or phone calls? What are the ground rules for overriding the covenant? If the covenant can be broken for an emergency, what constitutes an emergency? Some teams require everyone to be available for large portions of the day. Or sometimes people need to always be available for certain ministry areas, such as pastoral care emergencies. Whatever the rules, they should be made clear before people join the team.

The pandemic highlighted learnings about segmentors and integrators that are extremely helpful for building teams, even if almost everyone is back in the office. If a segmentor is forced to function as an integrator or vice versa, they will be miserable. The two types explain preferences that go to the heart of what makes a person happy and productive at work.

Working from Home Successfully

Whether a segmentor or an integrator, working from home successfully requires specific skills. Denise Mai, a self-described "digital nomad" who writes about living in ways that create personal freedom, has written an extremely helpful article on these skills:

+ You need to have A LOT of self-discipline.
+ You need to be able to stay focused and not get distracted easily.
+ You need to be great with time management.
+ You need to be organized and structured.
+ You need to be able to work on your own without constant supervision.

* You need to be ok with working alone and spending most of your day alone (or go to coworking spaces).[5]

From a managerial perspective, this list is helpful in allowing managers to evaluate who is likely to work successfully from home. For example, if an employee has difficulty with self-discipline in an office setting, they will definitely have trouble being productive working from home, where there are distractions galore. Or if an employee clearly benefits from the creative interaction with other staff members, the person will struggle at home unless there is an intentional strategy to keep the staff team connected so virtual conversation and brainstorming can take place.

Those who have trouble with time management will more likely struggle with working from home. Unfortunately, in my experience with clergy colleagues, time management is an issue in general, apart from work-at-home issues. I'm not sure clergy are worse at time management than other professions, but it is an issue. I am incredulous, at times, when a clergyperson tells me how much time they regularly spend on a sermon, devote to email correspondence, or pour into administrative tasks. They tell me about endless hours of work to explain why they are so overworked. However, when we talk more, what I often hear is poor time management, which translates into working more than a healthy number of hours. I'm sure many folks are working hard but not as sure that some of them are working smart in terms of time management.

Managers I interviewed said they spent a lot of time during the pandemic with a small number of staff members who were struggling to work at home. These staff members needed more, if not constant, supervision to keep them on track and satisfied. The managers described having to regularly remind such staff people about what the most important deliverable was and when it needed to be completed and to create short-term plans as to how to get the job done. During the pandemic, managers expressed reluctance to fire people because of the already high unemployment rates. However, in normal times, a staff member needing very high supervision is probably not a good fit for a staff position.

Whether we like or do not like, whether we are successful or unsuccessful, working from home is not a reflection on our character. It is simply a matter that requires self-knowledge and, for supervisors, awareness of whom they are managing. Just as many of us have gained important knowledge about ourselves from Myers-Briggs, so we can better understand ourselves if we think about the circumstances that make for our best work environment.

Creating a Work Day

While understanding our preferences for certain work environments is helpful, best practices can make the experience more successful for everyone. If I am correct that most congregations will adopt a hybrid work situation, where staff can work at home and in the office, organizing how and when that happens will be important. A team at the University of Zurich had discussions about how to order their workweek. They considered three categories: work from home, work at the office, and personal/family time. They concluded, "Our team invented a '3-2-2 week' that gives us a good balance: each week, we spend three days at the office (yes, we think the commute time is worth the conviviality that only the office can afford), two days working from home, and two days dedicated to family and friends."[6]

Much management literature, including Mai's article, stresses the need for people to set a daily schedule for themselves while working from home. For example, some of the parents with young children in my neighborhood who work from home split their childcare into two blocks, eight o'clock to noon and noon to four o'clock. One parent takes one block while the other parent works, and then they reverse roles. The parents cover for each other when they must work before eight o'clock or after four o'clock.

Of course, a recent Pew Research poll found 23 percent of the total US parenting population lives in single-parent households.[7] The challenges to a single-parent situation and the ability to create an interruption-free work zone can be even more challenging for single parents who have no one to manage the children while working. While childcare is an option, it is costly. Single-parent friends of mine say that they do work that requires total concentration after the kids go to sleep or before they wake up. They do other types of work during the day as they are able.

One of the key problems with working from home is the distraction factor. As I work with my clients and participate in various nonprofits' board meetings, I find people are adapting to children popping into the picture frame. In the early days of the pandemic, people felt a need to comment, "Oh, what a cute kid." As the pandemic continued, call participants became used to the presence of kids in their meetings and did not bother to note the child. Of course, the parent was distracted temporarily, but the meeting continued uninterrupted.

Still, we can be distracted by a myriad of things, ranging from pets to online surfing. Along with creating some type of daily and weekly schedule, establishing a distraction-free zone in a staff person's day is crucial to maintaining high productivity and quality work. This is especially important for the segmentors. Defining a time when a staff person is totally dedicated to work and can eliminate distractions, as much as possible, is crucial. In my interviews, I heard a widespread desire to return to the office, at least for part of the day, simply to be in a more controllable, less distracting environment.

An idea from the Zurich group helps create a sense of schedule and accomplishment. They schedule something every day that they consider a "must win." They advise, "If your to-do list is anything like ours, it is always too long. To avoid drowning in work, identify a must win for each day—one thing you need to achieve no matter what—and then pursue it at full steam."[8] They suggest such a strategy creates a sense of accomplishment each day. Frankly, this is a great approach to work whether one is working from home or in an office. But given the way everything can morph together when working from home, it feels especially important to have tangible accomplishments in virtual working situations. I have adopted it in my own life.

There is universal agreement in the literature that people need to take scheduled breaks during the day (preferably including some exercise, such as walking, during the breaks), leave the house periodically during the day, and create definite stop times for the workday. Every single person I interviewed complained of fatigue, not just with videoconferences but from sitting in front of a monitor for extended periods of time. If we don't take care of ourselves by adopting a fixed schedule, including breaks and days off, we will pay both a physical and a mental price.

Stay-at-home workers need to be sure to take sick and vacation days. Even though one's home becomes one's workplace for working-from-home employees, it does not mean that one necessarily has to travel to get the health benefits of a vacation. Boston University epidemiologist and mental health expert Sandro Galea advises, "The value of vacation is to remove the stressors of one's day-to-day engagements. . . . If that can be achieved through staying at home, it would have the same mental health benefit as going elsewhere."[9]

One final but important thing for congregational staff to do is have a spot online where every staff member's work and vacation schedule is posted. With one click, a staff member should be able to see whether a colleague is likely available to respond to a text or plan for their absence for a vacation. There are plenty of software options staff teams can use to post such information. Honoring one another's posted schedule will eliminate a lot of needless and damaging irritation within a team.

FOMO

In my research, I kept running across the acronym FOMO (fear of missing out). When people work from home, they worry that things are happening in their team or at the physical workplace about which they do not know. They grow concerned that their lack of knowledge of things will hurt their careers and impede their effectiveness.

I am not a psychologist. But I know that each of us, from an early age, has a fear of being left out. It happened in grammar school, in seminary, in the workplace, in retirement, and everywhere in between. I am so glad that scholars of the workplace have identified the FOMO phenomenon. Hopefully, we will begin to deal with it intentionally. Staff teams need to have explicit discussions about how they avoid FOMO by staying connected to one another while spending significant time away from the office. Who needs to know what and how will they be kept informed are key team discussions.

In fact, staff staying connected with one another has been an issue in congregations long before the internet age. There have always been congregational staff members who did not spend a lot of time at the office or, when they did, did not interact much with the rest of the staff. Early in my career, I worked on several staff teams where it was clear that some members definitely had little desire to be part of the team. Certainly, this is a person's right. But if the staff is going to be a team, everyone has to see one of their responsibilities as being an engaged teammate. When hiring, those doing the interviewing need to be explicit with candidates about what is expected of a staff teammate.

Having the Right Tools

Plumbers cannot do their jobs without possessing the proper tools. The same is true for congregational staffers. More than one-fifth of the way into the twenty-first century, some essential tools for ministry have been added to the toolbox. For example, adequate internet bandwidth is now indispensable. Everyone has been on a videoconference call where the sound or, more likely, the video keeps breaking up. When that happens, it is caused by one of two things: either we do not have enough internet bandwidth (speed) or someone else on the call does not have adequate speed. Whether working in the office, at home, or in a hybrid mode, to succeed, people need to have sufficient speed from their internet provider.

How much bandwidth do we need? Lincoln Lavoie, a senior engineer of broadband technologies, says, "[Bandwidth] depends more on the applications being used (streaming is largely a downstream application), but as users start doing more things like video calls and movie sharing, upload also becomes very important. Similarly, upload speeds are critical for people working remotely from home, as upload speeds would impact things like screen sharing and online conference calls."[10] Often we have no problems listening to a call (downloading), but others complain we are breaking up when we start to speak (uploading)—a sign that we do not have enough internet speed.

A key consideration when determining how much bandwidth we need relates to the number of devices using our internet connection. When we are working at home, if someone is likely to be streaming a movie on a TV screen while two teenagers are watching YouTube videos on their phones, we need more bandwidth than if we live alone. Most of the experts I consulted think 150–200 Mbps is best. This download speed will be accompanied by an upload speed high enough to avoid breaking up when speaking on a videoconference. But the level of service considered "basic" changes rapidly, so a congregation's and remote workers' services should be reviewed regularly.

Of course, it is also crucial not only that a congregation has high internet speeds in its buildings but that signals are widely available. Too often when I am consulting with a congregation, a team has gathered in a room where there is a problematic Wi-Fi connection, and the meeting quickly devolves. I recently talked with a pastor who had to keep moving around his office to find a strong signal. Having good Wi-Fi coverage in a church building is as essential today as having electricity in every room. Staff working in the office will need a strong internet connection to stay in touch with staff working from home.

A congregation's office and buildings can have huge bandwidth, but if the staff does not have adequate bandwidth at home, problems arise. As a result, I strongly recommend that congregations that will have staff working from home or in a hybrid mode give their employees a work-from-home allowance similar to travel and continuing education allowances currently offered by many congregations. Several of the managers I interviewed said they are already doing this for their staff. If we want people to work without the irritation and reduced productivity produced by slow internet speeds at home or inadequate workspaces and equipment, the employer, not the employee, needs to carry the burden of that cost. A home office allowance could also be used to upgrade an employee's laptop, desktop, monitor, or printer at home. It could even be used to purchase an ergonomic chair. During the pandemic, a growing body of literature said people working from home were developing back problems!

Most congregations have sensitive financial data on their members. It needs to be protected. Many congregations have found a virtual private network (VPN) connection to be a useful tool to create a secure, encrypted connection between workers at home and the office. While a VPN increases security, having excellent antivirus software is also crucial to reduce the risks of hacking, ransomware, or virus infection while working from home or elsewhere.

Ideally, congregations have moved their shared files from servers in their offices to the cloud. The hybrid worker benefits by having access to the same files whether at home or the office. This is essential for agile teamwork, where sharing files within a team is crucial. If a staffer does not work at a congregation that has moved to the cloud, the person needs to have a secure backup system (external hard drive or a personal cloud account) at home to ensure access to files if a computer crashes.

Returning to the Office

Working in the office will no longer be the default. I believe the hybrid work world—working from home as well as working at the office—will be standard for congregations for years to come. Each staff member's work location will be evaluated with the following question: "Can it be done at home as well as in the office?" If a person comes to the church office and sits in the office all day with little interaction or collaboration with the rest of the congregational staff or membership, why have the person in the building? The person can work just as well at home as sitting in isolation at the office. In the meantime, the staffer's office space can be designated for another valuable use.

Offices themselves have changed considerably over the past century. Businesses have tried separate offices, cubicles, and open office designs, and I have seen quite a few of the latter in my visits to consulting clients. Even before the pandemic, the latest versions of the open office had lost their appeal for an increasing number of employers. The open office negatives boil down to three key issues: lack of privacy, distractions, and . . . wait for it ... spread of disease. Yes, spread of disease in office spaces was a growing topic of discussion in office design even before the pandemic. Many congregation offices I visit have administrative staff members sitting together closely in a single open space. One synagogue with which I worked had four administrative assistants jammed (in my opinion) into a single room. Going forward, this will have to change.

A *Washington Post* article discussed what changes we can expect in postpandemic-era office space design. Brent Capron, design director of interiors for the architecture firm Perkins&Will, says, "I don't think the open office is dead, but I think we may have additional barriers for comfort. ... I've been calling it the 'sneeze guard effect.'"[11] Indeed, as the pandemic grew, in visits to any type of office, we found the presence of plastic barriers between workers and the public and between workers and workers. Those designing future offices will be placing a high priority on health concerns as they balance health safety with other priorities. An *Architect* article suggests the following trends for the near future: "Seating in conference rooms will not be so closely spaced, desks will be further apart, and staff may work in the office on a rotating schedule to keep the density lower."[12]

Moving forward, employees who have health vulnerabilities will surely be demanding increased safety precautions in congregational workplaces. Members and visitors to congregations will likely expect the same. "There will be another epidemic or another pandemic—or there might just be another flu season," says Eve Edelstein, cofounder of the research-based design consultancy Clinicians for Design. "Let's go ahead and design for that reality."[13]

Congregations should be evaluating the capacity of their HVAC systems to provide purified air as well as looking at ways to make buildings easier to access and get around without touch. For example, the use of automatic doors will increase, with doors activated by a sensor that only requires a hand waved in front of it. Hand sanitizer dispensers will be omnipresent. Cleaning staff will focus on doorknobs as never before. Creating safe distances between a receptionist or administrative assistant and those with whom they interact will be crucial.

Andrew Bennett, a design principal in a large architectural firm, says, "In this new normal, safe is not just about what a building code would tell you, that if there's a fire the sprinklers come on.... Now, it's this whole new spectrum of viruses and the well-being of people and the quality of the air that they get in their buildings and everything like that."[14] Interestingly, the modernist architecture movement in the 1930s was in response to another major health crisis: tuberculosis.[15] Design follows function!

Obviously, making office spaces safe and functional in a hybrid-working world will cost congregations money. However, if in the postpandemic era we become as germophobic as some analysts think we will, it will be a necessary expense. When considering the cost of improving health safety, we need to consider the cost of not doing it. Everyone I interviewed or have read agrees that postpandemic, people will have an increased reluctance to enter spaces they do not consider safe. If we want people to visit us (and we do!), we need to make the necessary upgrades.

A final key issue on offices relates to cleaning. One of my favorite quotes I came across while researching this book was from the *Washington Post* article "The Post-pandemic Workplace Will Hardly Look like the One We Left Behind": "'Traditionally, private desks haven't been cleaned very often,' says Kay Sargent, director of workplace at the architecture and design firm HOK, as housekeeping services are warned not to mess with precarious stacks of papers.'Most people's desks are dirtier than a toilet.'"[16] Before we scoff at that comment, let us remember that the dirtiest place on an airplane is not the toilet but the fold-down tray at our seats.[17]

The Hybrid World

I do not think people, in the future, will be working exclusively from home, despite some loud voices making that argument. Humans are social. It is not a coincidence that mental health problems rapidly escalated during the pandemic when we were isolated from others. A Kaiser Family Foundation poll reported one-half of Americans saying that the pandemic was harming their mental health.[18] A study on depression by Johann Hari found that isolated individuals were three times more likely to catch a cold than people having many close contacts with others.[19] Being isolated is literally not good for us.

As all my interviewees stressed, there is no way to replace the creative, cohesion-building environment of face-to-face work. Can work get done? Yes. Can it get done with high productivity rates? Yes. Is it as creative as having people meeting in the same room? That has yet to be definitively demonstrated. Is it as satisfying as working in close physical proximity with coworkers? For most of us, there is little to suggest that it is. Relationships can certainly be built virtually. But do they have the richness and depth of face-to-face relationships? In some situations, the answer can be yes, but in most situations, the answer is no.[20]

Consultants at McKinsey & Company, one of the most prestigious worldwide consulting firms, summarize some of the key questions facing us as we contemplate increased work from home: "Is it possible that the satisfaction and productivity people experience working from homes is the product of the social capital built up through countless hours of water-cooler conversations, meetings, and social engagements before the onset of the crisis? Will corporate cultures and communities erode over time without physical interaction? Will planned and unplanned moments of collaboration become impaired? Will there be less mentorship and talent development? Has working from home succeeded only because it is viewed as temporary, not permanent?"[21] All of these questions raise valid choices congregations need to consider as they think about the work model they want their staff members to use.

For congregations, there is an additional key issue. While I celebrate the many positive aspects of virtual work I have described in this book, I keep harkening back to something Rev. Ed Harding said to me in an interview. He told me that he "misses the touch. Ministry, John, is about touching people."[22] Ministry is about touching the disadvantaged in the world and touching the members and participants in our congregations. It is also about touching those with whom we work. Without the touch, we lose hold of one of the big reasons many of us go into ministry, why most people join or participate in a congregation. We want to be engaged with people.

Jerry Cannon, senior pastor of C. N. Jenkins Memorial Presbyterian Church in Charlotte, North Carolina, beautifully framed the issue about the lack of personal contact that dominates a time of pandemic. He said to me, "John, we have lost the secret sauce that makes congregational ministry so tasty."[23] Jerry described a universal sense of loss, among those I interviewed, over the dramatically diminished number of personal interactions between clergy and their members, staff, and the community. Pastors, ministers, rabbis, and priests suffered during the pandemic when they were deprived of personal interactions with their staff and members. After all, they are relationship experts at a time when it was challenging to put that expertise to work.

I watched 2020 Rosh Hashanah services online with my wife. The Temple Sinai (Washington, DC) staff did a remarkable job of replicating virtually the power of that ancient, gorgeous service. To achieve their goal, they spent considerable money on all the technological best practices available. What they could not do was replicate the joy we experience when sitting in the same seat at the temple, or the magic members who have worshipped together for decades feel as they greet each other with "Shana Tova," or the mystical power of people praying together from the prayer book. The liturgy, message, and music were there online. The "touch" was not. The missing touch is why hybrid work, working not only at home but at the office, is the future of work for both many congregational members in their secular jobs and congregational staff members. Touch is why congregations will want their staff back in the office for at least part of the week.

That being said, I am not suggesting that we return to what was. When I first went to Western Church in 1983, I visited each of the members in their homes. It was the way ministry was done by many of us in those days. By the time I retired in 2012, more than half the members were under the age of fifty, and many in the younger demographic did not want a home visit. Instead, they would ask, "How about having a cup of coffee near work, John?" or "How about getting together for lunch?" With the folks under the age of thirty, the response to a possible home visit was often, "Have I done something wrong?" or "I just don't have time. How about a phone call?" For most, the desire for the "touch" was still there, but touch meant different things to people of different demographics. While I adapted and had ever-increasing numbers of cups of coffee and lunches with members (gaining a lot of weight in the process), I knew I was retiring at the right time!

So, no, there is no going back to the way things were when it comes to a ministry that touches people. Today and in the future, it will increasingly have a digital component. The good news is that there are and will be more ways than ever to touch people.

While the transition away from home visitation to different ways of touching members was natural at Western Church as we attracted a large number of young people to the ministry, it is more challenging in most congregations today because of the older age of their members. For mainline denominations, the average age of participants is not going down; it is going up. The median age in the Presbyterian Church (USA) is fifty-nine; United Church of Christ (UCC), fifty-nine; Evangelical Lutheran Church of America, fifty-five; United Methodist Church, fifty-seven; and Episcopal Church, fifty-six. Remember, median means one-half of the members are over the ages I just listed. With membership numbers skewed to those approaching, at, or beyond retirement age, what does the reality of memberships growing older mean for congregations transitioning to the hybrid model of work, a model of work many in the older generation never experienced, do not want to experience, or retired to avoid?

I am convinced that many staff will get pushback from older generations as they move to the hybrid model and are not in the office as much as in the past. I can hear the comments now: "I went by the church to check on where I am on paying my pledge, and no one was there?" "When I called, I got a taped message saying I could find the relevant information in the online calendar on the website." "The pastor sent me a text message saying he was sorry about my recent fall." Far from being hypothetical, these are the sort of comments I have heard numerous times in strategic-planning meetings in my consulting work.

Being a boomer myself, I am not about to write off my peers. But boomers have grown used to one way of staff members performing their work, and it involves a lot of face-to-face interaction with the membership. Even if humans do not like something, we grow accustomed to what we experience and know. Therefore, we occasionally resist changing even things we do not necessarily like. Because the hybrid model is a change, moving to it has the potential to create conflict even for those who do not really care about it. They will defend continuing to work in a church office simply because it is what they are used to.

To minimize conflict and misunderstanding, transitioning to a hybrid model of staff work will require an intentional strategy by congregational leadership. As with any strategy for change, answers to the following questions need to be well communicated:

- Why are we allowing church staff to work from home more often? To answer this question effectively requires clarity of purpose—not just saying, "Some staff want to." It has to be rooted in a congregation's overall values regarding empowerment and care for its staff.
- How does this improve the effectiveness of our ministry? This book provides numerous answers to the question.
- How do we know people are actually working from home? Actually, the question we have to answer is, "How do we know people are working anywhere?" The answer lies in whatever systems of accountability we have created for our staff and volunteers.
- How will we be in touch with and touched by staff who are working more from home? This is probably the most important question of all. The staff and governing board need to answer this with specific examples of how staff will relate to the congregation in normal and crisis times.

I think all these questions are eminently fair. If we attempt the change to a hybrid model without explicit discussion with the members and staff, the questions will drone on and increase, undermining morale within the staff and among members.

Staff members will need to develop and publicize their work schedule, being clear about when they are working in the office, when they are at home, and how to get in touch with them in both places. Staff will need to be attentive to voice mail (from older members, especially) and text and email messages. There should be clarity with the congregation about the time frame in which members can expect a response from staff—one hour, twenty-four hours, and so on. What to do in cases of pastoral care emergencies must be crystal clear.

If a congregation has a well-thought-out, transparent strategy by which the staff and members understand who is working when and where, I see no reason trust cannot be maintained between the two. Distrust grows in the fertile soil of confusion. When people do not know what is happening and why it is happening, some will move to sinister explanations. Let us make sure our clarity shines a light on a path that creates trust.

QUESTIONS

1. Are you a segmentor or integrator? How does that impact your work? How does it affect your view of your colleagues? Your thoughts and feelings about your work?
2. Do you have the personal characteristics that make people effective when working from home? If so, which ones? If not, could you develop these characteristics?
3. Does your congregation provide the staff with the tools needed to work at home? If not, what tools would be needed for each staff person? Do you provide them with a healthy, safe workplace in their offices?
4. How will your congregation react as staff work more at home, leaving the congregation's office a less busy and less vibrant place?

Conclusion

I want to reiterate a point I made earlier: not everything is going to be different postpandemic. The core functions and teachings of a religious community will remain the same. As Bishop Craig Satterlee, bishop of the Evangelical Lutheran Church of America North/West Lower Michigan Synod, said to me, "For Lutherans, the church is where the Gospel is preached and the sacraments are administered according to the Gospel." For Jewish, Roman Catholic, or other types of congregations, comparable core functions lie at the heart of their lives. A lot of the work of a congregation flows from those core functions. Pastoral care, teaching the faith, leading worship, and mission to the community are a few of the ministries that flow from the core functions of a congregation. These core beliefs and practices are not going to change postpandemic—or ever.

How these functions are done will change. I doubt they will change as much as some prognosticators are predicting. For example, for the umpteenth time in my forty years of ministry, some are saying that buildings are extraneous to the work of a congregation. While they are not always necessary, they are sometimes absolutely essential.

I learned how valuable a building can be during my years serving Western Church. For example, when the homeless needed to be fed in the Foggy Bottom neighborhood in Washington, DC, in 1983, there was not one building or even one room in a building available in the area for this work. Our neighbors, religious and secular, did not see feeding the homeless as a core function. Western Church was the only place that made itself available and continues to do so to this day. Why? Feeding the homeless flowed out of a belief that a core function of the congregation is to care for the poor. As one ruling elder said, "I don't think it is a good idea to bring three hundred homeless people every day into our aging physical plant. But the Gospel doesn't give us any choice. It says the hungry must be fed. I vote to feed them."

Fifty years from now, I expect religious communities to look like this.

+ There will be fewer congregations, but most of the ones that remain will carry out their mission from a building. If they are smart, they will do so from a building they own because it is always cheaper long-term to own than rent, and owning will give congregations more control over their facility and, therefore, more control over their ministry.

+ Pastors, rabbis, priests, and other clergy will visit people in the hospital, design inspiring worship services, teach the faith, and manage mission programs that feed the hungry, heal the sick, and comfort those in need.

+ Clergy and lay leaders will spend time raising money to fund the ministries of their congregations.

+ Clergy will help families as they pass through life cycle moments, including baptisms, namings, first communions, bat/bar mitzvahs, confirmations, weddings and divorces, and diseases and deaths.

I say all of this to slow down, I hope, what I view as a rush to conclude that everything we have done for thousands of years is about to change. Forward-thinking energy companies are moving from fossil fuels to renewable energy sources, smart retailers are adding online options for customers, and automobile companies are moving from gasoline-fueled to battery-powered cars. Companies are still providing energy, retail, and automobile services to their customers. But how and what they provide changes with the times. So it must be for congregations. We need to stay focused on our core functions but be flexible in how we do them.

What We Can Learn from Managing in a Pandemic

If you accept my premise that the core mission of congregations remains the same, the first two chapters of this book are the most important. They describe core management principles that go back to the beginning of time. Whether we analyze Moses and Aaron managing their people as they traveled to the promised land or Jesus managing his disciples, core management principles can be observed at work. Effective managers set clear expectations, give people the freedom to do their jobs, and evaluate how successful they are in realizing the expectations. I would add that Moses and Jesus did a good job of "hiring" their staff!

Communication Is Key

When using core management principles and strategies virtually, one needs to attend to issues that are amplified in the virtual environment. Communication, important in every type of management, takes on even greater importance virtually than it does when people are working face-to-face. I have described numerous examples of rabbis and clergy who said they struggled with intrateam communications early in the pandemic period. As the pandemic proceeded, they realized the missing component was casual conversations that take place in the office. They talked about the issue, and each team came up with its own way of adapting. Even then, however, every clergyperson I interviewed said that communications were not as solid as when they had some face-to-face contact with staff teammates.

Noncongregational managers with whom I spoke, people who have been managing virtually for years, did not express the concerns about communications that the congregational managers had. They expressed no desire or need for face-to-face contact. Over the years, they have developed ways of watching for moments when communication may be less than optimum and calling it to the individual's or team's attention. They may observe a team or team member falling behind a schedule or teammates getting irritated with each other. Their favorite strategy was an old-fashioned individual phone call to find out why there was a problem.

Cynthia Vermillion-Foster, director of member services for the Unity denomination, managed her staff, located in Kansas City, virtually from Canada for more than a year before moving to Missouri. If there was even a hint of a problem, she was quick to get on the phone with staff members to see if she could help. Resolving issues before they become major problems is key to effective management.

Accountability Is Essential

During the pandemic, numerous congregational managers worried about how they could hold their staff and volunteer teams accountable. As they worried, I think they woke up to a problem that existed before going virtual—namely, too many congregations are essentially accountability-free zones. There is little attempt to hold staff or volunteers accountable for their work. Indeed, in some congregations, what they are supposed to do is not sufficiently defined. A person may be defined as a religious-education staffer, for example, but has no quantifiable deliverables.

At Western Church, a member, a senior official at the Pentagon, quit our governing board over accountability. He was dismayed that some of our volunteers were not doing their assignments and wanted to fire them. When I explained that firing them was not an option, he said, "John, I love you; I love the congregation. I'm not leaving the church. But I cannot be part of a governing body that cannot or will not hold people accountable." He had a point.

The transition to virtual management during the pandemic raised the accountability issue to a new level of awareness for managers and congregation members. For example, when there was no face-to-face Sunday school because of the pandemic, it led folks to ask what the religious educator was doing. Boo McCready, the talented director of Children's Spiritual Life at Church of the Atonement in Overland Park, Kansas, developed a number of programs in response to the pandemic. They enabled her and the team leader, senior pastor Zac Sturm, to measure the performance and participation of children in the congregation's program even though the kids were not physically at the church.

During the pandemic, worship was an area with increased attention to measurables. I was fascinated that more clergy were talking about "attendance" when worship was virtual than when it is face-to-face. Certainly, part of this notice was due to the novelty of online worship for some congregations. Of course, clergy wanted to know if anybody was tuning in. I would argue that clergy should be just as focused on how many people are attending face-to-face worship services. True, it is not the only metric to watch. But it is a deliverable. Like Bishop Satterlee, I find it impossible to imagine a future church where people are not attending worship in person.

All of this is to say that managing a congregation during the pandemic generated new attention to accountability. As congregations organize themselves in a postpandemic hybrid model, they need to remain focused on who among their staff teams and volunteers is doing what, when, and how well. This will be especially important if I am correct in my belief that some long-term, older members may be suspicious of staff who start spending large portions of their time working from home. I can hear the comment, "How do we know they are working when they are home?" As I have argued in this book, the real question is, "How do we know if they are working—at home or in the office?" Period.

One of the people I discussed, Bishop Oliveto, offers an answer. She understands the futility of trying to micromanage people in an area as large as the Rocky Mountains. Indeed, she understands the futility of trying to do it in her conference's central office. The way one achieves high performance is by holding people accountable for deliverables, which depends on asking the right questions. Do people deliver what they were asked to deliver? Do they deliver it on time? Do they deliver the quality of work product that is expected? Mindy Douglas, senior pastor at First Presbyterian Church in Durham, North Carolina, uses a powerful management tool: if a deliverable is not forthcoming, she talks with the staff person about what kind of help the person needs to get the job done. She has found that when staff view her as a source of help rather than a source of harsh judgment, they more readily seek her help rather than waiting until a disaster unfolds. Her strategy, in effect, encourages employees and volunteers to hold themselves accountable and ask for what they need.

Teams Work

The hybrid model will also solve some problems that appeared during the pandemic. I spend a lot of time writing about teams because, in the twenty-first century, effective congregations build and do their work with teams. A "sense of team" or team bonding is very important. During the pandemic period, the clergy I interviewed expressed a sense of weakening team bonds. Rabbi Jonathan Roos said his team was losing their "shared stories." My guess is that Rabbi Roos was quick to identify this loss because Judaism is a shared story of a people in a way few religions are. Lose the story and we lose the sense of being a people. With renewed face-to-face interaction, the hybrid model should restore what was lost in a strictly virtual time and create new stories in the future. Although Bishop Satterlee's team is predominately virtual, he still gathers them together regularly enough to keep them a cohesive, friendly group.

Solitude Is Useful

The move to a hybrid model is an excellent opportunity to debunk the mythology that an office is the best place to accomplish work. The shift to increased home-based work during the pandemic gave employers a penetrating look into which tasks can be done well from home and which are better accomplished in person. Eve Edelstein, cofounder of the consulting firm Clinicians for Design, says her research suggests that "individual work has always suffered in the traditional workplace, with its abundant distractions."[1]

I am not sure why Edelstein's insight is not better appreciated. Forever, many clergy, including me, have left the office to go home in an attempt to find some peace and quiet. Who can write a sermon with people regularly coming into our office with questions, conversations taking place in the hallway, or the front doorbell ringing? Some people can, but not most of us. Given the swirl of activity around a pastor's office, I am not even sure it is the best place for pastoral counseling and other tasks that require total concentration. As we live into the hybrid model, we need to explain the advantages of working from home to our staff and members alike. With the technology now available to keep us connected, working from the office and the home must be seen as positive options aligned with particular types of work.

Offices Matter

The hybrid model will require governing boards to think creatively about policies to guide managers, staff, and volunteers as they think through working from home. Would an injury sustained while working at home be eligible for workers' compensation? Would the congregation's liability insurance policies cover that worker? On what grounds would a supervisor write up a staff person for abusing work-from-home privileges? What type of allowance for internet and other tools should a congregation give to staff working significant hours from home? The list goes on.

I want to reiterate the importance of thinking creatively about church offices. Edelstein suggests we "turn them into carefully controlled spaces that people feel comfortable being in."[2] A huge amount of literature says that companies and other organizations will lose their clients and participants if work and gathering spaces are not perceived as healthy. I was talking with a clinical therapist who gave up her office during the pandemic because so many of her clients refused to go there. It had no windows that could be opened and an old, poorly maintained HVAC system. The clients preferred teletherapy to putting their health at risk in a dated office. These types of health and safety issues are going to impact congregations postpandemic.

Will every congregation have members who demand a healthy building? Surely not. However, enough people will be concerned that it will be highly detrimental to congregations not taking these issues seriously. You will remember me telling Western Church's janitor that he helped our church grow by keeping the nursery so clean because parents demand such a healthy environment for their children. Postpandemic, the same expectations will apply to the rest of the building. This is especially important given the predictions by many infectious disease experts that we are not done with pandemics and lesser major infectious disease outbreaks.[3]

Judicatories Go Virtual

Virtual management is helping denominational judicatories like those led by Bishops Oliveto and Satterlee. Bishop Satterlee reports that his synod staff is better able to stay in contact with congregational governing boards virtually than when face-to-face meetings were the only option. What used to entail a multihour drive for a judicatory staffer to a congregational meeting now takes place with a videoconference. Using virtual tools, congregations can better access resources (people, curriculum, templates for bylaws, and the like) from their denominations. Bishop Oliveto's conference uses virtual tools to connect people involved in specialized ministries, such as women, youth, and others scattered across the Rocky Mountains. Effective use of virtual tools should make judicatories that are always talking about connectionalism better connected!

Embracing Technology

Congregations do not have a choice about whether to use technology to serve their members and communities. To serve God in the twenty-first century, mastering technology is mandatory. Technology itself is a two-edged sword. It can cut and heal. We know that people had conflicting thoughts about the development of another two-edged sword: the printing press. Without it, the Reformation would probably have failed. Luther's ability to circulate his thinking in tracts was key to his success. However, many people, including the pope at the time of the Reformation, thought the printing press was the work of the devil. So people today have widely differing attitudes toward technology. Some congregations are putting their collective heads in the sand when it comes to technology, choosing to use it as little as possible; others are using it poorly; and some are becoming masters of the printing press of our day—the internet. The congregations seizing the power of technology will grow with it into the future.

My colleague Susan Beaumont, congregational consultant and author, is one of many experts and commentators urging congregations to reflect on what they learned during the pandemic. I recommend Beaumont's recent work as a helpful framework as congregations reflect on everything from the use of technology in ministry to how to engage younger generations.[4] Every clergyperson I interviewed six months into the pandemic said in-depth reflections were well underway in the congregations they served. I sense, however, that many other congregations are not having these conversations. It is my hope and prayer that this book will help congregations and clergy as they reflect on how best to embrace the technological tools that God is giving us to do God's work in the world.

Notes

Introduction

1 Ben Eisen, "Workers Are Fleeing Big Cities for Smaller Ones—and Taking Their Jobs with Them," *Wall Street Journal*, September 7, 2019, https://tinyurl.com/y3op8ohw.

2 Daniel Bortz, "How Your Professional Growth Can Benefit from Changing Jobs Every Four Years," Monster, accessed July 22, 2020, https://tinyurl.com/rpk9vp5; "Employee Tenure Summary," Economic News Release, US Bureau of Labor Statistics, September 22, 2020, https://www.bls.gov/news.release/tenure.nro.htm.

3 James McWhinney, "The Demise of the Defined-Benefit Plan," Investopedia, February 18, 2020, https://tinyurl.com/y2xvmd6q.

4 "Changes in the American Workplace," Pew Research Center, October 6, 2016, https://tinyurl.com/y6y4qu7q.

Chapter 1

1 Linda A. Hill, "Becoming the Boss," *Harvard Business Review*, January 2007, https://hbr.org/2007/01/becoming-the-boss.

2 Edwin Friedman, *Generation to Generation: Family Process in Church and Synagogue*, Guilford Family Therapy Series (New York: Guilford Press, 1985).

3 Leigh Bond, Zoom interview with author, July 20, 2020.

4 Dictionary.com, s.v. "talent (*n.*)," accessed January 26, 2020, https://www.dictionary.com/browse/talent.

5 Marcus Buckingham, "What Great Managers Do," *Harvard Business Review*, March 2005, https://hbr.org/2005/03/what-great-managers-do.

6 Laura Goode, "How Lifetime Became One of the Best Places in Hollywood for Women," BuzzFeed News, April 17, 2016, https://tinyurl.com/yyzhgncd.

7 Richard Fry, "Millennials Are the Largest Generation in the U.S. Labor Force," Pew Research Center, April 11, 2018, https://tinyurl.com/yylgoxtm.

8 Peter Economy, "The (Millennial) Workplace of the Future Is Almost Here—These 3 Things Are about to Change Big Time," *Inc.*, January 15, 2019, https://tinyurl.com/y9cxxkbd.

9 "How to Manage Different Generations," *Wall Street Journal*, How-To Guide, Managing Your People, accessed January 26, 2020, https://www.wsj.com/articles/workers-are-fleeing-big-cities-for-small-onesand-taking-their-jobs-with-them-11567848600 (URL inactive).

10 Daniel Steingold, "Survey: Most Millennials, Gen Z Adults Prefer Texting over Talking in Person," StudyFinds, October 18, 2017, https://tinyurl.com/yc7nfssu.

11 Jason Harney, "10 Ways to Improve Emotional Safety in the Workplace," HR.com, January 8, 2020, https://tinyurl.com/yyvf45rh.

12 Peter Cappelli and Anna Tavis, "The Performance Management Revolution," *Harvard Business Review*, October 2016, https://tinyurl.com/z5hfrm3.

13 NPR Staff, "Annual Job Review Is 'Total Baloney,' Expert Says," NPR, July 8, 2010, https://tinyurl.com/y22j9ka6.

14 Buckingham, "What Great Managers Do."

15 Buckingham, "What Great Managers Do."

Chapter 2

1 John W. Wimberly, *The Business of the Church: The Uncomfortable Truth That Faithful Ministry Requires Effective Management* (Lanham, MD: Rowman and Littlefield, 2010).

2 "2. Views about Religion in American Society," Pew Research Center: Religion and Public Life, March 12, 2020, https://tinyurl.com/yxgtzwfm.

3 Tomas Charorro-Premuzic, "Does Money Really Affect Motivation? A Review of the Research," *Harvard Business Review*, April 10, 2013, https://tinyurl.com/hmazbz3.

4 Dori Meinert, "How to Create Bulletproof Documentation," SHRM, July 1, 2016, https://tinyurl.com/y6f7xf2n.

5 Edgar H. Schein, *Organizational Culture and Leadership* (Hoboken, NJ: Wiley, 2010).

Chapter 3

1 Christopher Mims, "The Work-from-Home Shift Shocked Companies—Now They're Learning Its Lessons," *Wall Street Journal*, July 25, 2020, https://tinyurl.com/y5dwxoqw.

2 Mims.

3 Jon R. Katzenbach and Douglas K. Smith, "The Discipline of Teams," *Harvard Business Review*, July–August 2005, https://hbr.org/2005/07/the-discipline-of-teams.

4 Yael Zofi, *A Manager's Guide to Virtual Teams* (New York: Amacom, 2011), 52–53.

5 Zofi, 1.

6 Wanda Thibodeaux, "Why People Don't Make Phone Calls Anymore, according to Psychology," *Inc.*, November 30, 2018, https://tinyurl.com/yybn4ktc.

7 Prithwiraj (Raj) Choudhury, Barbara Z. Larson, and Cirrus Foroughi, "Is It Time to Let Employees Work from Anywhere?," *Harvard Business Review*, August 14, 2019, https://tinyurl.com/y2h9l2u8.

8 Zofi, *Manager's Guide*, 93.

9 Ed Harding, Zoom interview with author, August 3, 2020.

10 Choudhury, Larson, and Foroughi, "Is It Time?"

11 Ron Carruci, "To Retain New Hires, Spend More Time Onboarding Them," *Harvard Business Review*, December 3, 2018, https://tinyurl.com/y3joy8mc.

12 Jennifer Howard-Grenville, "How to Sustain Your Organization's Culture When Everyone Is Remote," *MIT Sloan Management Review*, June 24, 2020, https://tinyurl.com/y2d7s9re.

13 Howard-Grenville.

14 Howard-Grenville.

Chapter 4

1 Shannon Kershner, Zoom interview with author, October 28, 2020.

2 "Video: How Brainwriting Can Neutralize the Loudmouths," Northwestern Kellogg, accessed January 26, 2020, https://tinyurl.com/o7dcp5b.

3 Renee Cullinan, "Run Meetings That Are Fair to Introverts, Women, and Remote Workers," *Harvard Business Review*, April 29, 2016, https://tinyurl.com/y33llxmu.

4 Justin Hale and Joseph Grenny, "How to Get People to Actually Participate in Virtual Meetings," *Harvard Business Review*, March 9, 2020, https://tinyurl.com/y2lx8p3l.

5 Basecamp (website), accessed January 26, 2020, https://basecamp.com/.

6 Bruce Crandall, "To Focus Group, or Not to Focus Group?," Decision Analyst, accessed January 26, 2020, https://tinyurl.com/y4d4hxff.

Chapter 5

1 Jenna McGregor, "Remote Work Really Does Mean Longer Days—and More Meetings," *Washington Post*, August 4, 2020, https://tinyurl.com/y3s577cz.

2 Nancy P. Rothbard, "Building Work-Life Boundaries in the WFH Era," *Harvard Business Review*, July 15, 2020, https://tinyurl.com/y348hhg3.

3 Bob Felts, "Relationship George vs. Independent George," *Times-News*, Mary 22, 2013, https://tinyurl.com/yxlu4jn3. "In a conversation with Jerry Seinfeld he said, 'I have Relationship George. But there is also Independent George. That's the George you know, the George you grew up with ... Movie George, Coffee Shop George,

Liar George, Bawdy George.' Jerry responded, 'I love that George.' George replied, 'Me too, and he's dying. If Relationship George walks through this door, he will kill Independent George.'" Felts.

4 Lauren C. Howe, Ashley Whillans, and Jochen I. Menges, "How to (Actually) Save Time When You're Working Remotely," *Harvard Business Review*, August 24, 2020, https://tinyurl.com/y2xt5363.

5 Denise Mai, "21 Work from Home Pros and Cons—the Surprising Truth behind Remote Work," Digital Nomad Soul, September 6, 2020, https://tinyurl.com/yyardb9t.

6 Howe, Whillans, and Menges, "(Actually) Save Time."

7 Stephanie Kramer, "U.S. Has World's Highest Rate of Children Living in Single-Parent Households," Pew Research Center, December 12, 2019, https://tinyurl.com/ssfr7yc.

8 Howe, Whillans, and Menges, "(Actually) Save Time."

9 Shannon McMahon, "Traveling May Not Be Safe, but Leaving Vacation Days behind Isn't Healthy, Either," *Washington Post*, August 12, 2020, https://tinyurl.com/yxtt9kru.

10 Don Reisinger and Brian Westover, "What Internet Speed Do I Need? Here's How Many MBPS Is Enough," Tom's Guide, August 22, 2020, https://tinyurl.com/y6zhu7xm.

11 Jena McGregor, "The Post-pandemic Workplace Will Hardly Look like the One We Left Behind," *Washington Post*, April 23, 2020, https://tinyurl.com/y2q9vxr5.

12 Blaine Brownell, "Rethinking Office Design Trends in a Post-COVID World," *Architect*, May 18, 2020, https://tinyurl.com/yybr59wf.

13 Emily Vaughn, "Redesigning the Office for the Next 100-Year Flu (Yes, It's Coming)," NPR, September 14, 2020, https://tinyurl.com/yxz27akf.

14 Gabe Bullard, "How D.C.'s Workspaces Will Fundamentally Change after COVID-19," DCist, May 19, 2020, https://tinyurl.com/yxw7jzh7.

15 Kyle Chayka, "How the Coronavirus Will Reshape Architecture," *New Yorker*, June 17, 2020, https://tinyurl.com/ybltbxbd.

16 McGregor, "Post-pandemic Workplace."

17 Julia Zorthian, "5 of the Filthiest Places to Avoid on Airplanes," *Time*, August 7, 2017, https://tinyurl.com/tq27m2m.

18 Adam Gilbert Cnhi Indiana, "Mental Health Can Deteriorate during Pandemic," *News and Tribune*, July 30, 2020, https://tinyurl .com/y5e5y2ct.

19 Brownell, "Rethinking Office Design."

20 Brodie Boland, Aaron De Smet, Rob Palter, and Aditya Sanghvi, "Reimagining the Office and Work Life after COVID-19," McKinsey & Company, June 8, 2020, https://tinyurl.com/yap7zxgk.

21 Boland, De Smet, Palter, and Sanghvi.

22 Harding, Zoom interview.

23 Jerry Cannon, Zoom interview with author, October 9, 2020.

Conclusion

1 Boland, De Smet, Palter, and Sanghvi, "Reimagining the Office."

2 Boland, De Smet, Palter, and Sanghvi.

3 Victoria Gill, "Coronavirus: This Is Not the Last Pandemic," *BBC News*, June 6, 2020, https://tinyurl.com/y3bew7r6.

4 Susan Beaumont, "10 Questions to Ask Now," Susan Beaumont & Associates, June 19, 2020, https://tinyurl.com/yywa4xh4.

Recommended Resources

The following resources will enable readers to move deeper into specific topics addressed in this book.

Management

Friedman, Edwin H. *Generation to Generation: Family Process in Church and Synagogue*. Guilford Family Therapy Series. New York: Guilford Press, 1985.

>When an author captures the truth, that book is timeless. Such is the case with this classic by Ed Friedman. Along with Edgar Schein's *Organizational Culture and Leadership*, this exposition of family/congregational systems theory will help readers better understand why things happen in their congregations.

Harvard Business Review (HBR)

>This great monthly journal also offers an astounding archive of articles written over decades. Do a search for any issue we confront in managing our congregations, and *HBR* contains a wonderful collection of articles on the topic. An annual

subscription to the digital version is an affordable expenditure for a congregation or clergyperson.

Mintzberg, Henry. *Managing*. San Francisco: Berrett-Koehler, 2009.

> *Managing* is a very readable book by a scholar and consultant widely recognized as one of the world's top authorities on management. Mintzberg cites large studies and also examines real-life situations from his consulting work. I know of no book as comprehensive or insightful as *Managing*.

Schein, Edgar H. *Organizational Culture and Leadership*. 5th ed. Jossey-Bass Business and Management Series. Hoboken, NJ: Wiley, 2017.

> For many of us who study organizations, this is the bible regarding organizational culture and leadership. For clergy who want a deep dive into the causes of a congregation's behaviors, this is the book to read. Schein's analysis of the three-layered life of an organization is revelatory. His extensive case studies can be lengthy, but readers can skip them and stick to the broader principles.

Steinke, Peter L. *How Your Church Family Works: Understanding Congregations as Emotional Systems*. Lanham, MD: Rowman and Littlefield, 1993.

> Building on Friedman's work, Steinke offers wonderful examples of congregational systems theory applied to the behavior of a congregation, its members, and its staff.

Governance

Hotchkiss, Dan. *Governance and Ministry: Rethinking Board Leadership.* 2nd ed. Lanham, MD: Rowman and Littlefield, 2016.

Hotchkiss is a widely acknowledged authority on reforming congregational governance systems for the twenty-first century. Governance systems held over from the twentieth century typically exhaust the large numbers of volunteers required to staff them. Hotchkiss offers suggestions for leaner, more efficient governance systems.

Wimberly, John. *Mobilizing Congregations: How Teams Can Motivate Members and Get Things Done.* Lanham, MD: Rowman and Littlefield, 2015.

This book is a good companion to Hotchkiss's work. Getting younger generations to serve on committees is exceedingly difficult. However, they are very responsive to working on teams. It explains the difference between the committee- and team-driven models of ministry for the twenty-first century.

Technology

Books on technology become quickly outdated. Current sources for staying informed are *PC Magazine*, *Wired*, Digital Trends, and the *New York Times*'s technology section.